Delivering Digitally

Open and Distance Learning Series

Series Editor: Fred Lockwood

OPEN AND DISTANCE LEARNING SERIES

Delivering Digitally: Managing the Transition to the Knowledge Media

ALISTAIR INGLIS

PETER LING

VERA JOOSTEN

KOGAN PAGE

First published in 1999

Kogan Page Limited
120 Pentonville Road
London N1 9JN

British Library Cataloguing in Publication Data

A CIP record for this book is available from the British Library.

ISBN 0 7494 2933 X

Typeset by JS Typesetting, Wellingborough, Northants.
Printed and bound in Great Britain by Creative Print and Design (Wales), Ebbw Vale.

Contents

Series editor's foreword

In his book *Mega-Universities and Knowledge Media* published by Kogan Page, the Vice-Chancellor of the Open University (OU), Sir John Daniel, commented on the growth in the number of students studying online with the OU. His projection was for 30,000 students to be studying with the OU, via the new technologies, by 1998. This has proved to be an underestimate since at the start of the 1999 academic year the OU expects to have about 50,000 students studying for the whole or part of their course online – with more courses planned. More recently, Marc Eisenstadt and Tom Vincent, authors of *The Knowledge Web*, went on to explore and illustrate the impact of the knowledge media on education and training. *Delivering Digitally* complements these two books superbly.

Alistair Inglis, Peter Ling and Vera Joosten have assembled a book that provides managers and administrators, teachers and technicians, in fact anyone associated with the move to delivering teaching or training material digitally, with an invaluable resource. The need for such a book is clear. An inspection of the educational or training press will reveal increasing numbers of organizations in industry, commerce and the public services delivering material via the new technologies; the growth in this form of teaching and training is phenomenal. This book will make the transition from conventional teaching to digital forms of delivery less traumatic; it will identify the many aspects worthy of your attention and for you and your colleagues to resolve. The division into four self-contained sections will allow you to decide what is most relevant to you and let you decide the order in which you want to study the contents. Indeed, the detailed contents list, index and glossary will help you focus on the particular aspects that interest you most; even though I suspect you will find all of it interesting and that it repays any investment you make in its study.

This is not a book for technophobes. It does use the language of Communication & Information Technology (C&IT) and makes a strong case for the exploitation of the knowledge media. However, its clear focus is teaching and learning – using the knowledge media when it is most appropriate and to best effect. The authors' concern with assessing the cost effectiveness of any proposed investment in C&IT, of the required infrastructure to support it, investment in colleagues via staff development activities and its stringent evaluation sets them apart from most C&IT evangelists.

Alistair, Peter and Vera have displayed the best features of a team; combining their talents and providing a product that is broad in its scope, sufficiently detailed to address the main issues and yet packed with concrete advice. The models, frameworks and principles they offer, and the phases they describe in the transition to the knowledge media have emerged from careful research studies and some hard lessons in delivering digitally to adult learners in Australia – lessons from which we can all learn. With direction from these authors you have a better chance of getting there.

Fred Lockwood
January 1999

Preface

This book is designed for those with responsibilities for managing the transition from traditional approaches to education and training – whether face-to-face or at a distance – to forms of digital delivery. This includes everyone from the chief executive officers of educational and training organizations to heads of departments, course co-ordinators and technical and educational specialists.

This is not a book that needs to be read from cover to cover. We recognize that educational managers are busy individuals – especially those working to transform organizations. We have therefore tried to make its contents as accessible as possible. We have divided the book into four sections. Each more or less stands alone and may be read in isolation from the others.

The first section is for those who, as we do, like to put their policy and practice in context and to be able to support it with a theoretical position. The section provides a history of the emergence of knowledge media, an understanding of the social and educational contexts in which it is being adopted and an understanding of the learning and pedagogics appropriate to it.

The second section deals with the practicalities of *implementing the transition*. We start by examining one of the most important factors driving change at the present time – the matter of costs. We then contrast the implications for decision-making of treating expenditure as an investment rather than treating it as a cost. We move on to elements that require attention to effect the transition. These include re-engineering the technological infrastructure, re-skilling and supporting staff, reorienting the teaching programme, and redesigning learner support services. We provide guidance on developing an evaluation strategy which can be applied throughout the process. We conclude the section by indicating a sequence for effecting the transition.

The third section, on *quality assurance*, provides a framework for instituting quality assurance processes across all aspects of a digital delivery system.

The fourth and final section, on *the future*, takes a brief glance over the horizon to identify some of the new developments with which decision-makers will soon have to deal.

Terminology in this rapidly developing field is still being established. In keeping with other books in this series we have used the term 'knowledge media' originally coined by Marc Eisenstadt, Director of the Knowledge Institute at The Open University, to refer collectively to the digital delivery media, principally the World Wide Web and CD ROM. In places, we use the term 'new learning technologies' to refer specifically to the technologies supporting use of the knowledge media, such as Web servers and conferencing systems.

The original idea for this book arose from a research project undertaken by us for the Higher Educational Council in Australia – New Directions in Resource Based Learning: Quality, Costs and Access. The investigation was commissioned to inform the Council in offering advice to the Minister for Employment, Education and Training. A synopsis of that advice was published as the booklet *Quality in Resource Based Learning* (NBEET, 1997).

From our work on this project and from our experience in providing policy advice in an institution which is itself in the process of making the difficult transition to online delivery, we became aware of the challenge that many senior educational managers were facing. They are being confronted with managing aspects of the change process but often lack the technical, pedagogical, or economic knowledge they feel they require. It seemed that there was a need for a book that provided an easy-to-assimilate account of the major issues that arise and the key activities involved in making the transition to the knowledge media. We considered that such a book ought to set advice it offered within the relevant educational framework. Notwithstanding the breathtaking pace at which change is occurring, it is important that education and training managers base their decisions on sound rationales.

That was the concept. Fortunately Fred Lockwood and, in turn, Kogan Page, shared our conviction. However, as we got more deeply into the project we began to realize the enormity of the task we had set ourselves. The domain covers an extraordinarily wide range of topics, some of which have been the subject of whole books in this series. Unlike the authors of these other books, we have not been able to benefit from the work of years of research and practice. Distance educators are breaking much new ground in making the transition to delivery via the knowledge media.

We would have liked to have been able to 'practise what we preach' and had the product of our efforts evaluated in use. But the revolution is upon us and we must be content to draw on the best advice available if we are to participate in it. We are nevertheless keen to receive feedback from you, our readers, on how adequately we have met your needs and where you would have wished we had said more (or, for that matter, had said less). We welcome any suggestions you might like to make and encourage you to make contact with us if there are specific changes you would like to see in any future edition.

Acknowledgements

We would especially like to thank those who have taken the time to read and comment on successive drafts of portions of the book: Mike Brooks, Paul Fritz, Vincent Harkins, Anne Lennox, Brian Livingston, and Kate Patrick. We have greatly valued their comments, criticisms and suggestions. We want also to express our appreciation to Fred Lockwood for his constant advice and encouragement. We wish to thank the staff of Kogan Page for their tolerance when we failed to meet the impossibly short deadline we had set ourselves and for their helpful advice.

Alistair Inglis, Peter Ling and Vera Joosten

Section I: CONTEXT

Chapter I

The origins of the knowledge media

In this chapter we trace the several pathways of development that have led to the explosion of activity in the knowledge media. We show that, contrary to popular perception, the sudden growth of activity is not the result of some unexpected recent breakthrough but the result of a succession of developments that date back more than three decades.

Revolution or evolution?

Every so often a breakthrough in technology is achieved that transforms the way in which a particular function is performed. The development of the compact cassette was one such development. Within a few years of its first appearance, the compact cassette had made reel-to-reel recorders obsolete. In doing so it set the scene for the emergence of the new lifestyle concept of 'music on the move'.

The compact disc is another example of a breakthrough technology which, as it happened, emerged in the same industry. It made the vinyl record obsolete and opened up new functions for data storage on computer disk.

Yet today in the information industry we are seeing changes that dwarf those brought about in the music industry by development of either the compact cassette or the compact disc. Whether these changes are measured in terms of their speed or their extent, their impact has been far-reaching. It is now being felt in every part of society. In the popular press these changes are being attributed to the 'digital revolution'. However, this abstract term is a shorthand way of referring to a rapid succession of technological breakthroughs. Of these, one of the most recent has been the creation of the World Wide Web.

The World Wide Web has for the first time provided the general public with convenient access to the resources of the Internet in a visually appealing format. In doing so it has begun to change the way in which we access information.

The education and training community has been quick to grasp the significance of the Web's development. Educational innovators have begun to explore the Web's possibilities. However, the most remarkable development has been the way in which education and training providers have rushed to exploit the potential of the knowledge media. In an industry that is not noted for its willingness to embrace change, the enthusiasm with which the concept of online learning is being taken up by both teachers and administrators marks this as a watershed period.

Yet is it accurate to describe what is happening as a 'revolution'? Certainly the pace at which change is occurring would suggest that it is. Yet closer examination of the changes themselves suggests something else.

The shift to digital delivery of education and training programmes has been made possible, more than anything else, by the establishment of the World Wide Web. Yet the establishment of the Web is only one of several developments that explains this shift. In order to understand why the shift has come about we need to trace back through the sequence of historical developments that has brought us to this point.

To anyone who is not familiar with the history of computing it may seem that these developments have come upon us suddenly and unexpectedly. Yet, if we trace back the origins of each of these developments, we soon see that the seeds of this revolution were planted more than three decades ago.

The creation of the World Wide Web

The idea of the World Wide Web was the brainchild of Tim Berners-Lee at CERN, the European Laboratory for Particle Physics. Berners-Lee conceived of the Web as a convenient way of sharing documents over the Internet. The Internet was already well-established by this time; Berners-Lee transformed the Internet into the transport medium for hyperlinked documents.

The initial manifestation of the Web still required a certain amount of technical familiarity with computers and networking. What enabled people who did not have a technical background to gain access to the Web was the release of the first Web browser, Mosaic. Mosaic was developed by Marc Andreeson at the National Supercomputer Laboratory (NCSA) in the United States. It was made available to the public for downloading over the Internet at no charge. The first alpha version of Mosaic – for X Windows – was released in February 1993. In September 1993, working versions of Mosaic were released for Windows and Macintosh.

Even though it was slow and had very few of the features we all expect today, it immediately became popular.

The importance of Mosaic was that it gave the general public – even those with little knowledge of computing – the opportunity to get a glimpse of what the World Wide Web might have to offer. By December 1993, major articles analysing the likely significance of the World Wide Web had appeared in *The New York Times, The Guardian* and *The Economist*.

In March 1994, Andreeson left NCSA to found Mosaic Communications Corporation, which subsequently became Netscape Corporation. Two months later, the first international World Wide Web conference was held at CERN in Geneva.

Laying the foundations for the Web

The creation of the Web was quite simple in concept. It prescribed a set of standards by which documents created in one computer could be displayed on another thousands of kilometres away. Another set of standards specified how, by selecting a particular location in a document, a request would be issued for the retrieval of another from a document server anywhere on the Internet. These standards were embodied in two computer protocols:

- the Hypertext Transfer Protocol (HTTP); and
- the Hypertext Mark-up Language (HTML).

The creation of a hypertext distributed database depends on the definition of a standard set of rules for initiating the request for dispatch of a file when a 'hot link' is activated. HTTP is the set of standards that were adopted for this function to enable the World Wide Web to be set up.

HTML defines a set of formatting commands which allow the same materials to be displayed on different computers running different operating systems and equipped with screens of different resolution and size. HTML was actually not a completely new idea. It is a case of a document-based Standard Generalized Mark-up Language (SGML).

SGML had been developed as a mark-up language enabling text documents to be reproduced on different printers and typesetters. SGML has been in existence for many years. It was just starting to appear in word processing and page layout software at about the time the concept of the Web took hold.

The concept of hypertext

The creation of the World Wide Web depended on the concept of hypertext – text which expands not just in one or two dimensions but in multiple dimensions through links which connect a pointer in one document with another document which may be located somewhere else.

The concept of hypertext is not a new idea either. The term 'hypertext' was coined by Ted Nelson more than three decades ago. Nelson believed that the conventional methods of academic publishing could not survive much longer. He argued that the pressure to publish was exhausting the publishers' throughput capacity and the financial resources of the academic and research libraries. He suggested that the existing paper-based method of publishing would eventually be replaced by electronic methods. He proposed a system of electronic publishing based on distributed interconnected databases. Nelson's concept was based on an earlier idea called 'memex' that had been described by Vannevar Bush, science adviser to President Roosevelt during the Second World War (Bush, 1945). Bush was concerned that the vast amount of information that had been produced as a result of the research that had gone into the war effort should be available to scientists. He conceived of a device that could make links between related text and illustrations in different research publications.

Nelson established the Xanadu Project to develop his concept, and produced several prototypes of the Xanadu system. For a time, the Xanadu Project was supported financially by the Autocad Corporation. When Autocad decided to divest itself of projects not related to its core business of computer-aided drafting systems, Nelson was invited to move to Japan. However, the Xanadu Project was never fully commercialized.

The World Wide Web therefore constitutes the first fully implemented hypertext system. However, as it is presently being implemented, the Web violates several of the principles that Nelson enunciated for the design of hypertext systems. For example, Nelson considered that every document needed to be individually identified. On the Web, only sites are individually identified. Nelson also considered that, to avoid unreliability, copies of documents needed to be stored in several locations. However, the Web does not require a document to be duplicated. The effects of these and other changes are now starting to be felt. We shall return in the last chapter of this book to examine the main differences between Nelson's original hypertext concept and the way hypertext has been implemented in the World Wide Web and consider the implications that these differences are likely to have for the evolution of the Web.

Growth of the Internet

The concept of a distributed hypertext database can only be implemented in practice when there is a physical network linking the distributed server sites. The physical network that supports the World Wide Web is what we now know as the Internet. The Internet is not an integrated network like the local area network that an organization might install within a building. It is a myriad of links of all types interconnecting sites across the world. It comprises wire cables, optical cables, microwave links and even satellite uplinks. It interconnects tele-communication companies, universities, research organizations, government departments, Internet service providers and private individuals.

However, the Internet is not a particularly recent development either. Most major developed countries had the beginnings of the Internet at least a decade ago. In Australia this was called the Australian Academic and Research Network (AARNet), set up in 1989. In the United States, the National Science Foundation Network (NSFNet) was established in 1986. In Britain, the Joint Academic Network (JANET) was providing universities with a similar facility.

Yet even before the Internet came into existence there was an earlier network based on store-and-forward technologies. This was used to carry electronic mail.

The origins of the Internet can in fact be traced back as far as 1969. That was when the Advanced Research Projects Agency (ARPA) of the US Department of Defense set up ARPANet to connect military, university and defence con-tractors. For many years ARPANet had been used to exchange e-mail and data files, to access bulletin boards and library services. It was used to transport text, images and even computer software.

ARPANet was superseded by NFSNet in the mid-1980s. NFSNet was estab-lished by the National Science Foundations (NSF) to provide access for universities and other research organizations to the five supercomputer centres. NSF found that ARPANet was not able to provide the level of service required. However, NSFNet continued to use the same Internet protocol that ARPANet had established.

In 1987, NSFNet was upgraded in capacity and in 1992 it was upgraded again. In 1995 NSF began moving across to a backbone provided by a commercial network provider.

From this, admittedly brief, historical account it can be seen that the establish-ment of the World Wide Web represents the convergence of five separate pathways of technological development:

1. development of the concept of hypertext;
2. establishment of physical transport media – the Internet;
3. adoption of a common standard for communication – HTTP;
4. definition of a common standard for the formatting of Web pages – HTML; and
5. development of Web server and Web browser software.

As can be seen, the seeds of these developments were planted three decades ago. However, it took the intervening 30 years for these technologies to reach the stage of maturity that would allow the separate pathways of development to converge to produce what we call the World Wide Web. So, while in the press and in everyday conversation the World Wide Web and the Internet are often spoken about as if they are one and the same, an understanding of their historical origins makes it clear that they are quite separate entities.

Interactive multimedia

Advances in the area of interactive multimedia have not had quite so dramatic an impact as the developments associated with the Web. They could be more accurately described as 'evolutionary' rather than 'revolutionary'.

Development of the field of interactive multimedia followed closely on the heels of the development of the CD ROM. It has always been possible to do more on a local work station than across a network. The speed at which data can be moved from the floppy disk drive to the display of a desktop computer has always been faster than the speed at which data could be retrieved from a file server or from a mainframe computer. However, the factor that limited the potential of desktop computers was the amount of data that could be stored on portable storage media.

The development of optical disc technology completely changed that situation. At the time that the CD ROM disks became available not only could they store more than hundreds of floppy disks, they could also store more than typical hard drives. Their major limitation compared with floppy disks was that they were not a re–recordable medium. However, for the distribution of multimedia products this was an advantage rather than a disadvantage.

Optical disc technology

The physical medium of the CD ROM is the same as that used for audio CDs, though the way in which information is recorded on each is different. The fact that CD ROMs and audio CDs share the same physical medium has been critical to the success of CD ROM technology because it has enabled CD ROMs to be reproduced on the same presses used to reproduce audio CDs. This has led to the cost of reproducing CD ROMs falling much faster than would have been the case had optical discs been used for storage of computer data alone.

The optical recording technology on which they are based dates back to an earlier development – the laser videodisc player. Videodisc technology was originally developed by Phillips and Sony for home entertainment. It was intended to enable people to replay high quality movies in their homes. However, the videodisc never really caught on in the home entertainment market. It faced too much competition from the videotape recorder, which offered the advantage that it could record as well as replay.

However, an industrial version of the videodisc player, which could be interfaced to a computer was seen as offering a means of incorporating video into computer-delivered instruction. While this hybrid technology was somewhat clumsy to use, it was used by many education and training providers to develop innovative interactive multimedia programs. These early innovators then moved across to the use of CD ROM once this technology became available.

The field of interactive multimedia has therefore been evolving for more than 15 years.

Authoring systems

The recent growth of the field of interactive multimedia may be attributed in part to the availability of courseware authoring software, which gives the courseware developer who has no expertise in programming in high-level languages the ability to control the full range of presentation functions.

Most interactive multimedia courseware being produced today is developed using courseware-authoring software such as Asymetrix Toolbook, Adobe Authorware Professional or Macromedia Director in the case of Windows; or Apple Hypercard, Incwell Supercard, Adobe Authorware Professional or Macromedia Director in the case of the Macintosh. While use of these authoring packages calls for considerable skill if one is to produce worthwhile results, the level of expertise that is needed is by no means as great as would be required to program the same courseware in a high-level language such as C++. However, the use of courseware authoring systems does place restrictions on the features that can be incorporated into a courseware production.

The interactive multimedia courseware that is currently being produced falls into two broad categories – courseware for educational use, and courseware for product promotion. Interactive multimedia for educational purposes has much more demanding requirements than interactive multimedia for promotional purposes. The latter involves creative presentation, whereas the former needs to take into account the requirements of assessment.

Courseware authoring software has been evolving over a long period, yet in some respects it is still a relatively immature technology. Development of this class of software has tended to be focused on harnessing the presentation capabilities of microcomputers – providing the capabilities for replaying video, for producing animations, graphics and sound. Few of these systems have really adequate capabilities for testing student achievement or for monitoring students' progress.

Progress in the development of courseware authoring systems has paralleled the development of computers themselves. Courseware authoring systems only started to advance rapidly once the speed and storage capacity of computers made the replaying of video possible. Prior to that, the graphics capabilities of courseware authoring systems had limited graphics and animation. In tracing the development of courseware authoring systems, what one finds is that as the cost of computer technology has fallen, the labour cost of developing interactive multimedia courseware has not fallen correspondingly.

Computer-assisted instruction

In the early days of computing, the cost of computers was so high and their capabilities were so limited that their use for computer-assisted instruction was limited to the military and to well-endowed universities.

The PLATO Project at the University of Illinois at Urbana was one of the best known early examples of a computer-assisted instruction system. The success of the PLATO Project was due largely to its innovative use of technology. At a time when screen display units were only just becoming commonplace, the PLATO Project used specially designed graphics terminals employing touch screen technology. The PLATO Project also employed a team of dedicated programmers to develop the software upon which the system depended. This project represented a scale of investment which was beyond the resource capacities of most universities. Many universities and schools were nevertheless able to take advantage of the PLATO system by remotely accessing it over dial-up and dedicated connections. The PLATO system also spawned many other products that still occupy an important place today. Authorware Professional and Lotus Notes are two products that can trace their origins back to the PLATO Project.

Computer-managed learning

In the late 1970s a number of educators began to argue that while the cost of computers put computer-assisted instruction systems out of the reach of most teachers, most of the benefits of computers could be obtained if their use was limited to those functions for which they were most cost-effective, and traditional delivery media such as print, audio tape and video were used for the presentation of instruction. This hybrid approach became known as computer-managed learning (CML).

The functions that were performed by the computer in the case of these early CML systems included:

- tracking students' progress;
- testing students' achievement; and
- transmitting messages between students and teachers.

Instructions issued via the CML system told students which resource materials to study and when to study them.

The distinction between CML and CAL is still evident today. Courseware authoring packages exhibit their strengths in the area of presentation. To obtain a full range of computer testing functions, one generally has to turn to a software package specifically designed for CML. There is no technical reason why this should be so. It is a reflection of the stage of development of the courseware authoring systems and of the failure of the educational market to fully recognize the scope of their needs and to demand them of software developers.

The promise of expert systems

Two decades ago a great deal of interest was being shown in the development of expert systems which could monitor the progress of students and adjust the presentation of instruction accordingly. These were known as 'intelligent tutoring systems' and were based in part on artificial intelligence technology. However, this type of courseware authoring system did not at that time yield the results that had been expected of it. The problem lay in developing suitable user interfaces. In time, interest in intelligent tutoring systems waned. However, it did not disappear entirely. In recent times there has been a renewal of interest in this area and it is possible that with the much greater computing power that is now available in microcomputers we may see some breakthroughs.

Computer-mediated communication

The teaching of programmes offered by distance education and open learning has almost always involved a combination of packaged resource materials and teacher–student interaction. However, the importance given to each of these components differs widely. Some delivery models rely principally on the resource materials, and opportunities for teacher–student interaction are provided as a way of compensating for the inevitable deficiencies in what ideally would be a fully self-contained resource package. At the other end of the spectrum, teaching is conducted mainly through group interaction and such materials as are provided are designed to support this interaction and to provide a record of what transpired. Most examples of distance education and open learning programmes employ a balanced combination of these approaches.

The greater connectivity of telecommunications networks has led increasingly to an expectation among teachers that what they have been doing in the classroom they can now do at a distance and that this ability to extend the classroom across a country or across the world has all of a sudden made teaching at a distance more practicable.

'Computer-mediated communication' is the collective term now generally used to describe all forms of two-way interaction via computers. It includes:

- electronic mail (e-mail);
- asynchronous computer conferencing;
- synchronous computer conferencing; and
- video conferencing.

The use of e-mail has now become so widespread that it scarcely needs any explanation. The capabilities of electronic mail systems have evolved with the Internet and with software technology generally. In education and training, the first examples of the use of e-mail employed the MAIL facility built into the Unix operating system. MAIL was intended to allow computer programmers working on the same system to communicate with each other. However, with additional software, Unix MAIL was extended to allow mail to be delivered to other Unix systems over dial-up connections and leased lines via a store-and-forward process.

The main direction in which e-mail is now evolving is towards integration with other applications. For general users, e-mail is now being incorporated into the two most commonly used Web browsers – Netscape Navigator and Microsoft Internet Explorer. For business users, e-mail is being incorporated into groupware products such as Lotus Notes and Novell Groupwise.

Asynchronous computer conferencing involves interaction among a group of participants. Asynchronous conferencing may be supported by e-mail systems by arranging for every member of the group to set up the mail addresses of the group as a list of recipients. However, there are also a number of more specialized asynchronous conferencing systems.

The first example of the use of computers for conferencing was a simple tool that was built into the PLATO computer-assisted instruction system. The system became known as PLATO Notes. Software developers who worked on PLATO Notes subsequently adapted the concept to the business communication environment by developing Lotus Notes.

Lotus Notes is generally regarded as the leading example of groupware. However, Lotus Notes is a business application. It lacks many of the features required for educational use. Recognizing the potential size of the educational market, Lotus Corporation has adapted Lotus Notes for education as Learning Space.

In 1976, Turoff established the Electronic Information Exchange System (EIES) at the New Jersey Institute of Technology. EIES was initially set up to allow classroom discussion to continue throughout the semester. However, it subsequently gave rise to the development of a full-scale asynchronous conferencing service and to an online educational delivery system called the Virtual Classroom which still operates today. PLATO also gave birth to the first synchronous conferencing system. The most widely used example of synchronous conferencing is Internet Relay Chat (IRC).

Networked virtual environments (NVEs) offer a more sophisticated form of real-time communication than IRC and proprietary chat systems. These attempt to create virtual realities on the Internet. NVEs are of two types – Multi-user Object Oriented (MOO) environments which have defined structures, and Multi-user Dimension (MUD) environments which may be extended by participants. Early NVEs were text-only systems. However, NVEs have now been developed which provide full graphics environments. So far, the main use of NVEs has been for game playing; however, there has been some exploration of the application of NVEs for education and training.

The convergence of technologies

The World Wide Web, interactive multimedia and computer-mediated communication represent the three main streams of development in instructional technology. However, to continue to speak of these as if they represent separate domains is to maintain a distinction that is becoming increasingly false. As the technologies represented by the three streams of development evolved they also converged.

For many years, computer conferencing technology has been based on a client–server model. This is similar to the way in which e-mail systems are designed. Software on a central server collects, sorts, stores and distributes messages. Client software installed on the user's computer communicates with the server system to download and display or print out messages or to upload new messages to the system. However, the focus of development in this field in very recent time has shifted to the Web. Existing conferencing systems are being migrated to the Web and virtually all new conferencing systems are being designed for the Web. The two major Web browser developers, Netscape and Microsoft, have integrated conferencing functions into their browser interfaces.

Migration of computer conferencing to the Web represents a considerable compromise. The Web is designed to forward document files on request. Once a file has been forwarded, no connection remains between the Web browser and Web server. The way in which conferencing systems achieve interactivity on the Web is by using the Common Gateway Interface (CGI) protocol that is used to handle forms on the Web. The net result is that computer conferencing on the Web is much more tedious than it has been with client–server systems. However, the considerable attraction of having all services accessible from one interface will ensure that this trend continues.

The trend towards technological convergence can also be seen in relation to the technologies of courseware development. Word processing and desktop publishing packages such as Microsoft Word and Adobe Pagemaker now provide the capability to translate print documents to HTML. Similarly, multimedia authoring packages such as Asymetrix Toolbook and Macromedia Director allow multimedia productions to be delivered over the Web.

One distinction that still needs to be made is between local and online delivery of courseware. Today, a range of high capacity storage media is available for distribution of computer data. Recordable media include cartridge drives, ZIP discs, JAZ cartridges, write-once CD ROMs, magneto-optical discs and now DVD ROMs. Courseware may be distributed to distance education students via one of these media but then delivered from a local work station. Online delivery, as well as including delivery via Web pages, also includes delivery of text files in portable document format (PDF) for access by Adobe Acrobat, retrieval or despatch of documents via e-mail or file transfer protocol (FTP), and real-time streaming delivery of audio and video presentations.

Whether local or online delivery is to be preferred in a given situation depends on a large number of factors, most important of which will be the cost and quality of network communications that are available. However, this is not just a choice between one or the other. Courseware developers are increasingly recognizing that in most situations the best results can be achieved by combining local and online resources.

Having started with the concept of combining several media in a single package we are now moving to the point of combining multiple functions in a single medium. Multimedia is becoming unimedia.

Summary

The remarkable interest being shown in the potential of the knowledge media for use in education and training delivery cannot be explained in terms of a key technological breakthrough but rather in terms a series of developments that can be traced back over more than three decades. The most important of these developments have been:

- invention of the hypertext concept;
- building of the physical network connections that have given rise to the world-wide Internet;
- adoption of international standards for distribution and formatting of Web documents;
- development of more versatile software tools for courseware authoring;
- development of systems for supporting the range of teaching and learning activities of which a complete educational programme is comprised; and
- improvements in microprocessor, computer memory and disk storage technology that have enabled the sophistication of the tasks that can be carried out by computers to be greatly increased.

It is the cumulative effect of all of these developments, rather than a single major breakthrough, which has given rise to the situation we see today.

Chapter 2

Social forces driving educational change

In this chapter we examine the educational and social context in which the shift to knowledge media is taking place. We identify a variety of views about the distinguishing features of the current era and some consequences for educational institutions. We analyse the emerging expectation that digital media will enhance learning and accommodate the preferences and needs of the new clientele of post-school education and training. We conclude by identifying some educational policy implications with a focus on the use of knowledge media.

What is new in the world?

Post-secondary education operates in an era that has been characterized as a period of change to the point of disjunction with the structures and predictability of the 'modern' period of Western history. Features of the current period include:

- dynamic and continuous change and transformation;
- the failure of grand theories such as Marxism to locate and predict directions of change;
- the discontinuist and erratic rather than evolutionary nature of social change: the juxtaposition of various images of social, economic and political life and the transformation of images like Disneyworld, TV sports and Web pages into the realities with which we deal.

There is the rise of new social movements, giving a voice to others that were previously marginalized. There is the emergence of multiple new discourses, some arising directly from developments in information technologies, with terms such as 'synchronous and asynchronous communication', 'cyber cafes', 'netiquette', 'usergroups', etc. As a consequence the era can be seen as marked by personal and institutional searches for a new identity.

Is the current era different?

You have heard it said time and time again: 'This is the age of change. Today, nothing remains constant but change itself.' Yet is the change we are seeing fundamentally different from that which has gone before?

Radical change has surely been with us and with our forebears ever since the Enlightenment. The agrarian and industrial revolutions caused upheaval in day-to-day social life, in economic life and in politics. Now, at the turn of the millennium, can we say that the types of change that we are experiencing are any more radical than that which was experienced at the beginning of the twentieth century when machinery driven by steam, electricity and petroleum replaced manual and animal power? Is it more radical than moving from local self-sufficiency to national and international specialization?

Some would say we are experiencing a qualitatively different change – significantly different in pace. The current era is a period marked by restructures and transitions, in which social institutions, including education, are undergoing dynamic transformation.

Many labels have been given to the period. It has been called 'post-modern', 'post-Fordist', 'post-structural', 'post-capitalist', 'disorganized capitalist', 'post-industrial' and 'post-traditional'. Each of these labels carries the suggestion that the departure from the preceding era is a radical one. As Giddens (1991) puts it: 'Modern institutions differ from all preceding forms of social order in respect of their dynamism, the degree to which they undercut traditional habits and custom, and their global impact.'

A period of transition

For some social commentators, however, not all is adrift. Patterns and directions emerge, the major features being globalization and the breaking down of political and geographic boundaries as the borders for personal, corporate and institutional transactions. In the process of globalization, Western culture, particularly the market economy and Western science, have penetrated all societies (Drucker, 1993; Giddens, 1991; Wagner, 1994) and all social systems including higher education. Giddens labels the current era a period of high modernity, indicating a continuing if tenuous attachment to the modern era rather than the arrival of post-modernity.

Peter Drucker, the well-known analyst of business and social change, also does not see the quest of the West as being lost. Rather, what he sees is that some of the cherished forms are undergoing change. Drucker (1993: 195) talks about the 'post-capitalist' society. He sees this as being a society centred on knowledge. All work and all social interaction will have a cerebral dimension. One consequence of this change will be the demise of the working class. Post-capitalist society will require leadership by educated people who have access to the great heritage of the past and acquired a range of 'knowledges' that allows them to live in a world which is both increasingly globalized and increasingly tribalized.

Does it matter how we see the social context?

What is at issue is the way the world in which we live is perceived. Some people may perceive it as a modern, enlightened (in the sense of the Enlightenment) world susceptible to reason, to the determination of cause and effect and to predictability of outcomes. Others may perceive it as being only known through variable and personal interpretation in which image conflates with reality, boundaries cannot be maintained or even defined and discontinuity marks patterns and flows.

How we view the social environment makes a difference to our understanding of institutions, the way in which they function and their susceptibility to planned change. Holding a modern view of social institutions, it makes sense to study organizational psychology and to engage in scientific management. Holding a post-modern view, one could not define scientific principles of organizational behaviour. To effect change one would have to grasp the changing meanings, understanding and motivations of all those who constitute particular organizations.

The view we take in this book may be seen as somewhere between the modern and post-modern. Our premise is that social institutions are not entities with a life of their own, whose functions may be explained and controlled in terms of simple causes and effects. Organizations, rather, are concepts. They are constituted in the minds of people and therefore will be subject to different and variable interpretations and impressions and differing intensities of interest. On the other hand we recognize a good deal of commonality in our understanding of social institutions and of their physical environment and the way in which they operate – a sharing of meanings which allows us to proceed as though cause and effect were understandable and predictable.

The social analysis offered here suggests that we should not be surprised in the current era to find ourselves pulled in contrary directions. It also suggests, however, that it is valuable to work with common understanding, for instance, understanding of best practice in a particular field. And it suggests that it is not an appropriate response to simply abandon the old in favour of the new. A vision of worthwhile outcomes for education and careful consideration of the advantages and disadvantages of the various modes of attaining the outcomes provide a way to proceed. But best intentions and best practice are subject to the whims, understanding and actions of all players, and the actual outcomes of our endeavours may surprise us. There is no one best solution for all circumstances and all time

but there are some useful frames of reference for making judgements and inform-
ing actions.

Technology and the current era

Technology, particularly information technology, is the key component of the
change that characterizes the period. Globalization demands the breaching of
time and space limitations and draws upon information technology. At the same
time, technological development drives globalization. In arguments about whether
we are in a period of late modernity or whether we have entered a post-modern
period, information technology contributes to both sides.

On the one hand, information technology can be seen as creating a break
with the modern era. It is upsetting the types of relationships that previously
existed in time and space. It is breaking down borders. It is increasing faceless
encounters. Yet information technology relies on science from the modern era
for its development. It is in turn a vehicle for the dissemination of scientific
knowledge. The pursuit of order and of 'scientific' explanations still continues.
The mission of modernity is therefore not yet dead.

Educational institutions in the current era

In educational institutions, as in other institutions in society, traditional purposes
and modes of operation are being challenged and changed. In the process of this
change, the people who define and constitute institutions are caught up in a
transition between eras, which can lead to widespread confusion, alienation, anger
and, in some cases, apathy. It can also have the effect of excitement and challenge,
sparking creativity and the development of innovative approaches and strategies.
Both of these responses apply to the last decade of the twentieth century. In this
context it is not surprising that education, along with all other sectors of society,
is undergoing major transformation, rationalization, restructure and redefinition.
In a transition period such as this, social processes such as education are dynamic,
disjointed and discontinuous in their development.

The changing scene in post-secondary education

In higher education, institutions currently styled as universities have not come
from a unitary origin, being based on models as diverse as Oxford and Cambridge
universities, Scottish universities, German universities, technical colleges, schools
of mines, working men's colleges and other quite plebeian institutions. They may
soon head again in different directions in response to changing circumstances,
including changing teaching and learning technologies.

The traditional view that higher education services are best provided on a campus, to a student body resident nearby, via a narrow set of delivery methodologies... will come under increasing scrutiny... as the new technologies continue to expand the possibilities for location-independent interactions between teachers, between teachers and students, between students, and between students and the providers of academic support services.

(*Higher Education Review*, 1997: 9)

The idea of a university has changed over time. Cardinal Newman, writing from the Oxford perspective, saw the university of the 1840s as the vehicle for the conservation of knowledge and its transmission to an élite. Research was a matter for some other institution (Newman, reprint 1947).

Abraham Flexner, in the 1930s, referring to American, English and German universities, saw the university as advancing knowledge and studying problems as well as engaging in 'training' at the highest level (Flexner, reprint 1968).

Clark Kerr, reflecting in the 1960s on the writing of Flexner, saw the university as a pluralistic organization: 'Flexner did not realize how many functions can be combined into a single university – even apparently inconsistent functions' (Foreword by Kerr in Flexner, 1968: xviii).

From the nineteenth century, as Glenys Patterson points out, universities faced pressure for 'increasing democratization of access [and] pressures to be more responsive to the requirements of the industrial age' (Patterson, 1989: 5). Flexner had denied a place for practical training, admitting only the learned professions of medicine and law and denying 'the make believe professions' (Flexner, 1968: 45). How far we have shifted! Universities now are expected to demonstrate a strong commitment to 'enabling our graduates to play a productive, wealth–creating role in a modern, outwardly oriented economy' (*Higher Education Review*, 1997: 3). That which does not serve a practical economic end is hard to justify in the activities of universities. They have moved from élite to popular institutions; they will move to serving a mass market.

Kerr observed that Flexner did not appreciate the populist drive for education nor 'the desire of a technological society for knowledge' (Flexner, 1968: xix). Now the desire of a technological society for knowledge is translating into an arrangement for technologically acquired knowledge. This is the new imperative:

Our eyes are being opened to extraordinary possibilities in the provision of education through ever expanding technological advance.... New learning technologies must be eagerly embraced to cater for a far more diverse – and more discriminating – student body.

(*Higher Education Review*, 1997: vii)

The features of the emerging higher education institutions have been classed as a 'paradigm shift' in higher education by Kathy Tiano (cited in Australian Vice-Chancellors' Committee, 1996: 9) whose characterization of the old and new paradigms appears in Table 2.1.

Table 2.1   *Old and new paradigms of higher education, Kathy Tiano (cited in AVCC 1996:9)*

Old paradigm for higher education	New paradigm for higher education
Take what you can get	Courses on demand
Academic calendar	Year-round operations
University as a city	University as idea
Terminal degree	Lifelong learning
University as ivory tower	University as partner in society
Student = 18 to 25-year-old	Cradle to grave
Books are primary medium	Information on demand
Tenure	Market value
Single product	Information reuse/info exhaust
Student as a 'pain'	Student as a customer
Delivery in classroom	Delivery anywhere
Multicultural	Global
Bricks and mortar	Bits & bytes
Single discipline	Multi-discipline
Institution-centric	Market-centric
Government funded	Market funded
Technology as an expense	Technology as differentiator

Increasing flexibility in education and training

In the new world of education and training there has developed a conventional wisdom about the capacity of the digital media to enhance learning or to accommodate learner convenience and preferences. Digital courseware, by which we mean tuition materials developed for delivery by digital media such as CD ROM or the Internet, in conjunction with digital communication media such as e-mail, chat facilities and computer conferencing, has the potential to offer increased flexibility with respect to:

- place;
- time;
- pace;
- entry;
- exit.

Place

Online computing, floppy disks, CDs, videos and electronic conferencing by telephone, television or desktop computer may be accessed in libraries, in laboratories, in the workplace, in the home – anywhere where the appropriate technology is available.

Time

Digital storage media such as hard disks and floppy disks, CDs, Web sites, e-mail and videos may be accessed at a time convenient to the learner. Time flexibility is limited by the desirability of synchronous communication. Optimizing time flexibility is a matter of carefully considering what can be dealt with through one-way communication, what can be dealt with through asynchronous communication and what needs to be dealt with synchronously. One-way presentation or stand-alone materials maximize time flexibility. Asynchronous communication gives greater flexibility than synchronous. Of course there are considerations other than time flexibility in deciding upon the form of communication to be employed but if time flexibility is important then we might adopt as our default position stand-alone materials or asynchronous modes of communication.

Pace

Learning programmes utilizing electronic storage systems, like print-based materials before them, allow learners to proceed at their own pace. There may be reason to limit this flexibility, for example to accommodate time-constrained elements of the learning programme such as group activities, or for occupational requirements. Sometimes having a limited period of time to respond is seen as important to meeting assessment requirements or as important to simulating real-world conditions. Nevertheless digital media will usually allow the user greater freedom in pace than class attendance modes of study.

Entry

Where designed with alternative paths or modules, digitally based learning programmes can readily accommodate prior learning and offer alternative entry points, possibly based on an incorporated pre-test of understanding or competencies.

Exit

Digitally based learning programmes may also be constructed to allow users to pursue a topic to different depths or levels of proficiency, to select alternative topics, paths or sequences and to dip in and out of the programme.

Some issues facing post-secondary education

The major issues facing post-secondary education in the USA and Europe in the current era have been identified in national and OECD reports (National Board of Employment, Education and Training, 1996; National Information

Infrastructure Taskforce, 1994; OECD, 1996). In a 'user pays' environment, equity of access to education and training, the cost-effectiveness of modes of provision and the quality of education and training available are seen as major concerns. We can identify a number of issues relating to these trends.

The demand for education and training can be expected to increase beyond the capacity to provide it by traditional means. Even if it were desirable to respond to increased demand through the construction of traditional institutions it would be neither practical nor economic to do so.

The demand stems in part from the knowledge explosion. The more the use of technology is expanded to provide access to knowledge the more rapid and far reaching the knowledge explosion. There is an associated need for global information infrastructure standards and conventions and possibly a need for national or global assessment via networked services.

New forms of access are required to provide time and place flexibility, especially for adults as they engage in lifelong changes to work and social life. As these are adopted, some traditional distinctions in forms of provision of education and training are breaking down. The distinction between distance and attendance modes of educational provision is blurring or being redefined to allow flexible responses to education and training demands. The distinction between public and private providers will blur or be redefined with the privatization of public institutions in the era of the market economy, and the development of substantial enterprise-based on-the-job training. As public institutions embrace new modes of delivery, including online delivery and workplace-based education and training, their traditional roles as providers are challenged. Some may become service brokers or accrediting agencies rather than providers.

Approaches need to be found to transform individual and small-scale initiatives involving the new learning technologies into institutional and systemic change. There has often been a failure to move innovations from the innovators and early adopters of innovation to institution or system-wide application. On the other hand, the desirability of applying technological educational innovations more widely cannot be taken for granted. Many innovations are not systematically evaluated. Evaluations are most often conducted and reported by people with a vested interest in the innovation. The quality of some evaluations that have taken place is dubious. Most investigations of new learning technologies indicate no significant difference in learning outcomes where new technologies are employed.

The implications of trends for policy making

In concluding this chapter we advance some policy implications of trends in the current context and in education and training practice.

As part of the study for the Higher Education Council from which the idea for this book arose, we attempted to derive a set of policy implications for educational decision makers from current social and educational trends. We went

Table 2.2 *Premises and policy implications relating to the current context*

Premises	Policy implications
Economic and social change is generating new demands for lifelong learning which will not be satisfied in terms of quantity, quality or convenience by traditional attendance programmes	Adopting new approaches to the provision of education and training, including the utilization of new learning technologies, is not an option – it is an imperative
Public educational providers are becoming market driven. There is no longer a monopoly on education provision. End-users of post-secondary education and training are demanding services more responsive to their requirements	Education providers in the public sector, like those in the private sector, must be concerned with competition, costs and productivity
The demand for electronically delivered education and training will grow exponentially over the next decade as technological and market developments alter workforce requirements with increasing rapidity	The pace of developments in the use of educational technologies is such that universities and colleges risk losing relevance if they wait for the results of longitudinal research before making an investment in electronically mediated learning; rather they need to rely upon understandings of best practice
The distinction between on-campus and off-campus programmes continues but is diminishing. Off-campus programmes employ, as they have done for some time, face-to-face tutorials and laboratory work, and residential sessions. Now programmes for attending students increasingly employ strategies with time and place flexibility such as syndicate work, use of distance education materials, use of television and video materials and of computer-mediated instruction programmes. They also use the World Wide Web, e-mail and groupware. Workplace-based education and training provides a new definition of campus	Institutional organization, policies and procedures need to adapt to the learner as client who will sometimes and for some courses wish to learn on-campus, sometimes wish to learn in the workplace and sometimes wish to learn free of an prespecified location. The learner may wish to use the educational resources of the provider without having to attend timetabled classes. This has implications for student administration as well as for the provisions for learning. It may suggest new approaches to organization
The availability and use of new technologies for the provision of education and the extent of change in educational processes can be overstated. In the USA the National Information Infrastructure Task Force (1994) found that the way Americans teach, learn, transmit and access information remains largely unchanged from a century ago	While contextual factors suggest an imperative for rapid and substantial change, institutions need to be wary of adopting procedures and approaches to learning which are untried, which are not accessible to potential learners or which are not demanded or preferred by clients. Providers may attempt to lead the market

Table 2.2 *(continued)*

Premises	Policy implications
Face-to-face classes, many of them large lectures, remain the mainstream form of tuition	Those who wish to follow the more cautious approach of responding to the market need to research both the demands of the market and the capacity of clients to take up the educational technologies envisaged
Client expectations and government policies and procedures demand greater accountability and reporting	Given public accountability and market expectations, universities must find ways to evaluate qualitative and quantitative outcomes of electronically mediated learning. Quality outcomes cannot be assured by quality inputs such as campus facilities nor can universities rely on high tertiary entrance scores of school-leavers to ensure quality outcomes

Table 2.3 *Premises and policy implications relating to technical developments*

Premises	Policy implications
Where the resource material supplementing face-to-face teaching and learning has been largely print-based (eg, textbooks, reference books and journals), accessed through purchase, libraries and photocopying, students and teachers will increasingly make use of network-based means for sharing knowledge	The provision of on-campus facilities for access to print-based materials needs to be de-emphasized and provision of electronically accessed materials such as databases on CD ROM or online needs to be emphasized. The definition of libraries may need to change along with the relationship between libraries and computing services
	The applicability of any copyright fair dealing concessions (which apply to print) to digitized material requires clarification along with copyright and intellectual property rights for material developed by a provider
Much greater use can made of digital technologies in post-secondary education than at present. Strategies employing the new knowledge media can contribute effectively to most learning situations	Design, development and operational arrangements for digital learning resources need to be such that desired learning outcomes are clarified, an appropriate educational design and media mix are employed and learner support services are provided

Table 2.3   *(continued)*

Premises	Policy implications
	Development of digital learning resources must be driven primarily by educational principles, rather than by technological capacity
Technology alone will not solve the problems of increasing access to higher education	Education and training institutions need also to provide for flexible admission policies, recognition of prior learning, communication with potential clients, and the appropriate sharing of cost burdens
In many institutions developments in the new knowledge media are ad hoc, occurring through individual creative endeavours rather than as a consequence of strategic and systematic planning. The record of producing substantial change through encouragement of small scale innovations is not good	The demands for a significant shift in the modes of education and training provision suggest institution-wide or substantial changes are made rather than generating change through individual initiative. Committed leadership and the development of staff are essential to integrate the new technologies into mainstream teaching and learning
Existing university and inter-university information technology infrastructure will not accommodate the development of good quality digitally based programs on a large scale	The implication of large scale use of new knowledge media for infrastructure requirements needs to be determined. Decisions about communications hardware and software within institutions providing education and training need to be taken in conjunction with decisions about educational infrastructure requirements

about this by locating descriptors of the current social and educational context and descriptors of best practice in technology-mediated resource-based learning from the print literature and from sources published on the Web. We validated these by submitting them to a panel of approximately 30 experts in technology-mediated resource-based learning. We then derived a set of policy implications from the descriptors and sought validation of these from the same group of experts. Tables 2.2 to 2.5 show the descriptors and policy implications that we arrived at through this process.

Summary

We live in an era of great change, but every era since the Enlightenment has been seen as such. What makes this era different is the nature of the change.

Table 2.4 *Premises and policy implications relating to costs and benefits*

Premises	Policy implications
It has been proposed that digital educational resources are heavy on development costs and light on delivery costs while traditional face-to-face education is light on development costs and heavy on delivery costs. This proposition should not be accepted at face value. Costing studies suggest the economies of scale for use of the new knowledge media plateau after a critical enrolment is reached. The development and operational costs do not suggest that the new knowledge media can offer a cheaper means of providing effectively for the current levels of enrolment	Providers need to cost digital media carefully taking into account processes for educational effectiveness, such as direct or indirect interaction between teacher and learner and between learner and learner, which constitutes a continuing operational expense additional to development costs
While digital media offer prospects for improvement in the quality of higher education and for the capacity to deal with larger enrolments in higher education subjects, most research into knowledge media initiatives has failed to find any significant difference in learning outcomes between traditional and digitally based innovations	A policy to adopt new knowledge media needs to be based on a premise other than improvement in the quality of education and training provision unless a case can be made for the particular form of media to be adopted
Development and operational costs for digital technologies can be high	In an increasingly competitive market-place educational providers need to collaborate in the development of digitally based resources and in their utilization

The key factor now driving change is technology. Technology is creating a break with the modern era, breaking down borders and increasing globalization. Globalization requires technology, but developments in technology are also driving globalization.

As society changes, education and training providers are also being required to change. In both education and training there is a shift to offering greater flexibility – in relation to place, time, pace, entry and exit.

Education and training providers are also being expected to accommodate increased demand for education and new forms of access in the context of a rapid explosion in knowledge. They must contend with a blurring of the distinction between public and private providers and between distance and attendance modes of tuition.

Table 2.5 *Premises and policy implications relating to access and equity*

Premises	Policy implications
The benefits of utilizing the new knowledge media include a capacity to customize programmes, the accommodation of individual learning styles and individual student goals, and time and place convenience for both students and staff	The imperative to provide flexibility in the delivery arrangements for education and training suggests the development of educational provision policies which specify the potential benefits of the new knowledge media
The effects upon equity target groups of the introduction of new technologies into education and training programmes are not clear but the limited access which these target groups have to personal computing in the home indicates that they may be relatively further disadvantaged	Policy and provision arrangements need to provide for learners who do not have home, work or community access to the hardware and software required to use the new knowledge media
Access to university programmes for students reliant upon programmes offered by digital media is limited by the bias in the range of courses available toward humanities and business rather than science and technology	Education and training providers may need to make special provision to encourage the development of digital educational resources in technological and scientific areas

There are policy implications arising from this changing education and training environment. The digital age requires change at the institutional and system level if the current providers of education and training are to survive. Accountability considerations and market expectations demand responses to the needs and preferences of learners and quality assurance mechanisms. A focus on flexibility in provision needs to be accompanied by a determination to employ sound educational principles in the design and development of learning resources.

Chapter 3

Learning in an electronic environment

In this chapter we examine what we mean by 'learning'. We argue that for learning to be effective it needs to involve the active participation of the learner. We specify what our understanding of the nature of learning implies for the way we should view teaching. We then consider the implications that our conception of effective teaching has for the types of components that need to be built into an electronic learning environment if it is to support the learner adequately.

What is learning?

In the traditional model of the classroom, the teacher is the focus, standing in front of a group of students and presenting information. What the teacher does in this situation is sometimes described as 'communicate' knowledge. However, this explanation betrays a misunderstanding of what may actually be going on. Knowledge cannot simply be transmitted from teacher to student. A learner does not receive knowledge but rather constructs it. What a teacher transmits is information. When learners receive that information they construct knowledge from it.

This traditional approach to classroom teaching could be said to be based on a 'knowledge transfer' conception of teaching. It has been severely criticized on educational grounds because, when it is used in conjunction with forms of assessment which require recall, it encourages rote memorization. In so doing, it leads to surface understanding – a type of understanding in which more attention is paid to the words that are being spoken than the underlying significance of what is said.

Teaching by presenting verbal information can lead to rote memorization and surface learning but it need not necessarily do so. David Ausubel made the important distinction between rote memorization and meaningful verbal learning, either of which, he pointed out, could result from expository teaching. According to Ausubel, the key to enabling learners to engage in meaningful verbal learning is to present information in a sequence which enables them to use that information to extend their knowledge structures (Ausubel, 1963). Expository teaching which is sequenced so as to support meaningful verbal learning reflects a somewhat different, 'information transfer', conception of teaching.

The limitation of the 'information transfer' conception of teaching is that it supports the construction of only one type of knowledge – what we might call 'theoretical' knowledge. Where the 'information transfer' conception of teaching goes wrong is that it assumes that the only knowledge worth acquiring is theoretical knowledge. It may go further – it may assume that the only theoretical knowledge worth acquiring is that which is coincident with some particular 'expert' interpretation of a field of knowledge that is presented to learners in the context of their formal studies.

What does it mean to be expert?

Education and training is concerned with enabling learners to become expert in a particular field of endeavour. A person who is expert is a person who has a sophisticated understanding of a subject and displays the ability to act appropriately in practical situations.

A person's expertise may be judged by his or her actions. However, it cannot be assumed that a person who is able to act appropriately in one situation will be able to act appropriately in all situations. A person's capabilities are context-specific.

What do we mean by 'theory'?

Theoretical knowledge is knowledge comprised of theories. A theory is a way of understanding how the world and the things that comprise it work. The value of theories is that they enable us to make sense of information available to us and to anticipate events rather than having them unfold in ways we don't expect. By anticipating events we can act in ways that are more appropriate than the ways in which we are likely to act by intuition.

In formal education, the accent until recently has been on the acquisition of explicit or 'book' knowledge, especially in the case of university education. Most formal education takes the position that a person acquires the ability to act appropriately in a situation by developing a sound theoretical understanding of that situation. There is an assumption in that position that if people have acquired a theoretical understanding of a situation, then, when confronted with the need to deal with a problem in that situation, they will act according to their theoretical understanding. However, we know that in practice that isn't what happens. We can all think of situations where we have had the information base to have acted in a particular way but we have done something else. We have acted against our best judgement. What happens in those situations?

'Espoused theories' and 'theories-in-use'

Much of traditional educational practice reflects this implied assumption that if a person understands and accepts the validity of a theory then he or she will act according to its precepts. Many years ago the noted management theorists Chris Argyris and Donald Schön pointed out the fallacy of assuming that people invariably act according the theories they espouse (Argyris and Schön, 1974). They said that it was important to distinguish between the theory a person claims to embrace and the theory that was implied by their actions. They termed the latter a 'theory-in-use'.

The distinction between espoused theories and theories-in-use shifts the focus from the information that a person has been given to the knowledge he or she has acquired. An espoused theory is a theory that a person is able to describe. It constitutes a part of his or her explicit knowledge. One might assume that it would also be a theory that has gained acceptance among relevant experts. However, this need not necessarily be the case. It may be a misconstruction of an accepted theory or it could be a theory generated by the person him- or herself.

A theory-in-use is not an actual theory – that is, a theory which has been thought through and enunciated – but a theory that may be inferred from a person's actions.

Tacit knowledge

Action that is not sourced from espoused theory is sourced from tacit knowledge (Polanyi, 1958, 1967). Tacit knowledge is not the sort of book knowledge which is acquired through formal education. Tacit knowledge is that knowledge which we acquire through our experience of acting in the world. It is the type of knowledge that lets us recognize the face of someone we know. It is also the type of knowledge that gives rise to intuition and imagination. The value of tacit knowledge is that it is available to people even without their having made the decision to acquire it.

In everyday life, we rely on tacit knowledge most of the time. We act automatically, without thinking, in response to the world as it occurs for us. The problem with relying on tacit knowledge is that our 'automatic' behaviour may not always be appropriate. Once it has become automatic we will continue to exhibit it even in situations where it is inappropriate. To be able to act appropriately in the ever-changing situations of life we need to be able to disengage from our automatic way of responding and begin reflecting on the way in which we act in particular contexts in relation to possible alternative ways of acting.

Acting without thinking is not the mark of the uneducated person. On the contrary, one of the characteristics of an expert is that he or she is able to act quickly without thinking about what needs to be done. Experts' actions, too, are largely automatic. Their competence has reached a level at which their actions are sourced from tacit rather than theoretical knowledge. As their tacit knowledge of a situation continues to deepen, their mastery of the situation increases.

Theory and action

While the possession of theoretical knowledge may be accorded status as an indicator of achievement, theoretical knowledge is ultimately only of value if it can be applied in action. The value of theoretical knowledge is that it can guide our actions when we move into a new context or when the circumstances change. However, our use of newly acquired theoretical knowledge has to compete with long established behaviour. This is why, when people return to acting in the 'real world' after having completed a course of study, they will often revert to their old ways of doing things. Their tacit knowledge of the context calls forth their automatic response before they have had the opportunity to make a more considered assessment of the situation.

To enable people to act appropriately in many situations it is often necessary, therefore, to begin the process of aligning their tacit knowledge of the relevant context with their new-found theoretical knowledge. This restructuring of tacit knowledge is accomplished by applying the theory in practice. Such application of theory therefore constitutes part – indeed, it could be argued, the most important part – of the educational process.

Education therefore involves an interplay between theory and practice. The acquisition of theory informs the development of practice and the experience provides an opportunity for aligning tacit with theoretical knowledge. Education can go wrong where it separates theory and practice and/or places a barrier between them such that this interplay can no longer occur.

Action-oriented learning

The attention given by Schön (1983) and others to the importance of tacit knowledge in the attainment of professional competence has in more recent times led to a shift in professional education towards the adoption of action-oriented modes of learning. These include action learning (McGill and Beaty, 1992), situated learning (Seely *et al.*, 1989), and problem-based learning (Boud and Feletti, 1991). Such approaches have, however, often been adopted at the expense of theoretical knowledge.

What constitutes good teaching?

A simple definition of good teaching is that it is that which supports effective learning. We can therefore judge the quality of teaching by looking at the ways in which it supports learning.

If learning involves the acquisition of tacit and theoretical knowledge, then teaching must include the creation of opportunities for the development of both of these types of knowledge.

Considered at one level we can say that teaching should be directed at creating opportunities to develop the ability to act appropriately within a particular domain of action. Considered at a deeper level, we could say that teaching ought to involve providing the contexts in which learners can acquire both the tacit and the conceptual knowledge from which appropriate action arises.

In the case of the acquisition of theoretical knowledge, learning will involve acquisition of the theoretical frameworks in terms of which real-world situations are described. Good teaching will involve explicating these theoretical frameworks in ways which are meaningful, given the learner's already-acquired theoretical knowledge, and provide the learner with the opportunity to relate these theoretical frameworks to practical experience.

In the case of tacit knowledge, learning will involve gaining experience at acting in authentic situations. Teaching will involve providing the student with situations in which such experience can be obtained. This practice is what confers on learners the ability to put their newly gained theoretical and tacit knowledge to use. These opportunities may be provided by creating opportunities for practice at engaging with problems, issues and situations. They may also be provided by supplying rich learning environments created through the use of multimedia.

One implication of the conclusion that knowledge is constructed is that learners will construct their knowledge differently. This makes the design of stand-alone learning materials difficult. It implies that good teaching will also make provision for some degree of on-going teacher–learner interaction, whether at a distance or face-to-face.

Conceptions of teaching reflected in traditional distance education

Distance education uses different delivery methods from face-to-face classroom teaching. For much of the time students work independently. Even when they are engaged in face-to-face interaction it is for short intensive periods at weekend or residential schools or in study groups. Despite these differences, the way distance education and training programmes are delivered indicates the same range of understandings of teaching as can be recognized in face-to-face teaching.

On the one hand, one major group of distance educators sees the most important element of a distance education programme as being the learning package. Of these, there are some who still manifest the 'knowledge transfer' conception of teaching. The learning packages they provide typically comprise mainly subject matter information, but the information often displays comparatively little structuring. Fortunately, this group is shrinking in size. Those members of this group who manifest the 'information transfer' conception of teaching produce learning packages that are also substantially made up of subject matter information. However, in their case the information is carefully sequenced and extensive use is made of textual clues such as a hierarchy of headings and subheadings, typeface variations and other forms of signposting to reinforce the structure which is implicit in the text. Finally, there are those who consider that learning occurs primarily through doing. These distance educators build extensive interaction into their materials. Their materials are oriented towards having the learner attain defined learning outcomes and these outcomes are frequently expressed as competencies.

The other major group of distance educators sees the most important element of a programme as the discourse that occurs both between the tutor and the student and among the students themselves. For them the most important component of the teaching is the opportunities that are provided for students to interact. Among this group it is once again possible to discern three subgroups. There are those who see interaction as supporting the personal construction of knowledge (Garrison, 1993, 1995). Secondly, there are those who see knowledge as being constructed in a social context and interaction being necessary in order to provide that context (Evans and Nation, 1989). Finally, there are those who see interaction as challenging students' existing understandings, opening the way for students to make conceptual shifts (Laurillard, 1993).

The distinctions that have been drawn here reflect marked tendencies rather than clear divisions. While those who favour the use of learning packages consider that ideally the learning package ought to be self-contained, they nevertheless acknowledge that in practice this ideal can seldom be attained. They accept that the learning package must therefore be backed up by a range of other means of delivery, such as tele-tutorials, weekend and residential workshops, local study groups and individual access to tutors. This group of distance educators tends to see learning as the development of a student's capabilities in directions defined by the teacher. For them, the learning package serves to provide the resources needed to achieve this result.

Meanwhile, those who favour the use of interactive modes of delivery nevertheless generally accept the practical and economic necessity of making use of learning resources. They argue, though, that learning materials need to be used in such a way as to construct a dialogue between the teacher and the student.

In this connection, it is important to distinguish between the physical delivery of the package and metaphorical delivery of the course. In print-based distance education all the materials are assembled into an integrated package and the package mailed to students at the beginning of the study period. From the point of view of the physical package, delivery is mainly one-way. Yet experienced distance educators are acutely aware of the importance of incorporating activities into the design of learning packages. What happens to the physical package therefore tends to disguise a complex set of interactions that are engendered between the teacher and the student. Through the medium of the package, opportunities for interaction can be incorporated into programmes that are carried via a one-way delivery medium such as print. Even the language that is used in the package can help to create the experience of interacting with the tutor, rather than simply being the passive recipient of information.

At the other end of the spectrum there are programmes which are oriented entirely to project work where the package serves simply as a means of guiding the student to start and pursue the work.

So, the quality of the student's learning experience resides more in the way a medium has been used than in the characteristics of the medium itself.

Conceptions of electronic learning

If you browse through the recent literature on distance education and open learning you will notice the distinction that has been drawn between the use of the delivery media to support the communication of information and the use of the delivery media to support person-to-person interaction. There are those who see the role of online learning in terms of the delivery of Web-based materials. There are others who see the value of technology as lying in its capacity to support interaction between teachers and students and between student and student.

As in the case of traditional distance education, there are staunch advocates for both approaches. While programmes involve a combination of both approaches, they also tend to favour one approach or the other. Our view is that there is no single best approach to online delivery. The approach that is most appropriate in each situation will depend on a range of factors such as the nature of the subject, the backgrounds of the learners, the outcomes being sought, and the context in which the programme is being offered.

The approach that a teacher chooses to use in a particular situation will depend in part on the range of options that are available. It will generally only be possible to consider using a particular delivery method if the systems and procedures to support that method have already been put in place. The implication for providers of the adoption of a balanced approach to digital course delivery is that they need to be planning to support a spectrum of delivery options. We shall look more closely at what this might entail in Chapter 8.

In moving to embrace the knowledge media providers need to devise policies, systems and organizational structures which encourage teachers and trainers to adopt good practices and discourage them from adopting poor ones.

How should technology be used to support learning?

The way in which we see technology being used to support learning depends on how we conceive learning. If we conceive learning as the acquisition of book knowledge, then we will tend to view technology as providing a means of transmitting and presenting information. We will compare different technologies in terms of their ability to present information or their cost and the speed with which information can be moved from place to place.

If we conceive learning as occurring principally through the interaction between teacher and student and of students among themselves, then we will tend to view the value of technology in terms of its potential to support such interaction.

Why switch to the knowledge media?

Why might education and training providers want to make the transition to the knowledge media? Essentially there are three reasons. The knowledge media offer the possibility of delivering course in ways that are:

- cheaper;
- faster;
- better.

Cheaper

Many education and training providers are starting to make the transition to delivery via the digital media because they believe they can save on costs. In Chapter 4 we will examine more closely the issues that govern the costs of delivery in resource-based learning and how these are likely to be affected by a shift to the Web and multimedia. We point out there that whether it is cheaper to deliver via the digital media is not clear cut. However, we go on to explain that we believe the costs are certain to decrease with time and we explain why. Therefore, even though it may not yet be cheaper to deliver courses digitally, it will be before too long. The cost benefits of making the transition will accrue within the life of materials that are presently being developed.

Faster

Communication via the Internet has the potential to be almost instantaneous. When a hot link on a Web page is activated, it can result in an HTTP command being issued to the server on which the relevant document resides to download the document immediately. The server may be located halfway around the world.

This factor is important if you are delivering to students who are very distant – especially to students who are located in other countries. In this case the time taken for delivery of materials and especially for delivery and return of assignments can be very considerable. Use of the Internet can eliminate this delay.

Better

The primary reasons most education and training providers are shifting to the knowledge media may be to save cost, or to reduce delays in delivery. However, experienced distance educators consider that the most justifiable reason for considering such a shift is to improve the quality of the programmes that are offered.

The factors that affect the quality of a programme may be associated with the presentation of the learning materials, with the academic and administrative support provided to students, or with the type of interaction that is possible between teacher and student and among the students themselves.

Quality can also be interpreted as being related to the range of variation that is possible in the presentation of learning materials. Multimedia and Web-based material may be judged by some teachers as better because it offers a much more diverse range of presentation options including:

- colour;
- high quality halftones;
- animation;
- video;
- multimedia interaction;
- interaction between individuals;
- group interaction.

The role of information technology

Using the term 'information technology' to describe aspects of the delivery of education and training programmes can be misleading. It suggests that the function of the technology is to transmit information.

In the education and training literature one sometimes finds information technology that is used in an educational context being referred to as 'educational technology'. This usage is also misleading. The word 'technology' in the term 'educational technology' does not refer to hardware or software but rather to sets of principles used in designing materials.

Choosing the right term to describe information technology when it is applied to education and training is probably less important than recognizing that the role of information technology in education goes well beyond the mere delivery of information. Even when the technology is serving to transmit information, the information being transmitted is structured in particular ways so as to achieve educational purposes. It is the way that the information is structured that is of greatest importance here, not the speed or accuracy with which the information is carried from point to point.

It is unfortunately the case that many educational multimedia programmes do not conform to sound pedagogical principles. Many do little more than present large volumes of information – much of it textual. There is little reason to believe that students are motivated more strongly, or learn more effectively by reading information from a screen than by reading information from print. Simply from the point of view of cost, the use of multimedia for 'electronic page turning' needs to be challenged. This constitutes a very extravagant use of a particularly expensive medium. It would be much more economical to provide this information in print or even to include a copy of the document on a CD ROM in a form ready for printing.

However, the fact that many productions do little more than transmit information should not be regarded as a limitation of the medium itself. Rather, it is a matter of an inappropriate use of the medium.

Alternatives to the information dissemination model of electronic delivery

Over the past 20 years a number of instructional models have been developed for the design of courseware in computer-assisted learning. These include:

- drill and practice – learners respond to questions;
- tutorials – presentation of information via computer;
- simulations – learners are presented with a real-world situation to which they are required to react;
- problem solving – learners are given a problem situation and asked to find a solution.

All these models have now been adapted for use in interactive multimedia. However, up until recently, the range of instructional models that it was possible to implement in an online environment was limited by the range of software available for Web-based delivery of interactive multimedia products. As server systems become more sophisticated and Web browser plug-ins for interactive multimedia authoring systems become available, these facilities are quickly being exploited by courseware developers.

However, it is important to recognize that the delivery of distance education programmes involves much more than the delivery of learning resource materials.

What functions does an electronic learning environment need to support?

Educational institutions and training providers with no experience in delivering programmes at a distance often display too narrow a conception of what constitutes an adequate delivery system. They focus on the most obvious aspects of course delivery and ignore the ancillary support functions that help to ensure that learners complete their courses of study.

Delivery of a programme at a distance no more stops with the provision of the courseware or the conduct of online conferences than the delivery of a programme taught face-to-face stops with the conduct of the lectures and tutorials. A programme is not complete without appropriate assessment, tutorial, library and administrative support.

In making the transition to the knowledge media it is also important to consider how functions that previously would have been performed on a person-to-person basis ought to be conducted online. A system for supporting online learning therefore needs to support both teaching and learning functions and administrative functions:

- enrolment/registration of students;
- provision of course advice;
- provision of course materials;
- provision of feedback;
- provision of responses to administrative and academic queries;
- conduct of assessment;
- provision of assessment results.

In moving to the delivery of open and distance education programmes via the knowledge media it may be necessary to create new components of the organization's delivery systems or to adapt existing components.

Cost is a very important determinant of which technologies have reached a sufficient level of maturity to be considered for use in a production environment. It is always more expensive to conduct the trial of a technological innovation than it is to put the technology to use on a day-to-day basis. However, there are high ongoing costs in the adoption of some technologies.

With the escalation in the pace of innovation, the time that elapses between when a technology first appears and when it is ready to be taken up by education and training may be reducing. Nevertheless the basic principle remains.

Avoiding the risks of being oversold on technology

The success of innovations owes much to the pioneering work of early adopters. An early adopter sees an opportunity for a new way of accomplishing some outcome and sets out to demonstrate that it is possible. Early adopters gain satisfaction from being early and from having other people follow their example.

Early adopters feel that they can afford to take the risk of pursuing innovations that do not work out as expected. Indeed, part of their success comes from finding ways through the many barriers that pioneering a new application throws up. However, early adopters tend to highlight the advantages of innovation and to down play the disadvantages or limitations.

A technology which is ripe for exploration by early adopters may still be too immature for incorporation into a full production system. A favourite saying in the information technology industry is that the first users of a new piece of software become the test group that finds the software 'bugs'. The fact that a technology is capable of performing a particular function should not be taken to imply that it will be effective in performing that function from an educational point of view.

Recent advances in computer and communications technology are throwing up many exciting possibilities for improving the way in which education and training programmes are delivered. Yet managers of educational delivery systems require technologies which are functional, reliable and above all cost-effective. The technologies that are most effective in performing a particular delivery function are not necessarily those that are perceived to be the most 'glamorous' or 'hi-tech'. Often it is the simpler technology that, because of its greater reliability and lower cost, does the job.

The fields of education and training have generally not been at the forefront in the take-up of new technologies. Throughout the history of instructional technology, the technologies that have proven to be most successful have first found a market elsewhere. The compact cassette, the VHS cartridge and the overhead projector are all technologies that became established in entertainment or business first. Once they had secured a market there, educators saw the potential for adapting them to educational functions. The reason for this pattern is that widespread market adoption of a technology drives the cost down. Early adopters of a technology fund the recovery of the initial investment in research and development. With a few notable exceptions, fields of education and training have seldom had the resources to support the research and development costs needed to bring a new piece of technology onto the market. Moreover, education and training providers generally look for technology that is reliable and can be applied with some confidence.

For technology to support learning effectively it needs to support the full range of delivery functions. These include administrative functions such as enrolling and re-enrolling, provision of examination information and query handling. Supporting these functions requires the provision of a wider range of support functions. Distance educators are accustomed to thinking of the development of support systems holistically; teachers who are exclusively involved in teaching face-to-face are not. They tend to be more focused on the teaching-learning aspects of delivery. They do not have a lot to do with other support functions such as enrolment, examination, counselling. Yet all of these other functions need to be catered for by a system.

How effective is electronic delivery?

Distance educators have worked hard to overcome distance education's early reputation for high drop-out and failure rates. The key to reducing the incidence of drop-out and failure, it was found, was to improve the quality of the learning environment. It would be unfortunate if in making the transition from print-based to electronic delivery these hard-won gains were lost. It was not that print was an inappropriate medium for distance education but that print was not being used in a way that was appropriate to the needs of distance learners.

The development of interactive multimedia follows on from three decades of experience in computer-assisted instruction (CAI) and computer-managed learning. During this period a considerable amount of research has been undertaken into the effectiveness of computer-delivered education and training. An assessment of the early studies of the effectiveness of CAI concluded that computer-delivered instruction could be as effective as traditional instruction (Kulik et al., 1980). Later studies by the same researchers supported these early findings (Kulik and Kulik, 1986, 1991).

Multimedia does, of course, offer a range of more powerful capabilities than traditional computer-assisted instruction and computer-managed learning. It would therefore be reasonable to expect interactive multimedia to be potentially more effective.

In the short time that the World Wide Web has been functioning there has not been the opportunity for well-designed studies to be undertaken into its effectiveness compared with other forms of computer-based delivery or indeed compared with other forms of resource-based learning.

As was explained in Chapter 1, while the systems of computer conferencing that are being used today may be quite new, conferencing via computer was first introduced into education in the mid-1970s. Since then it has become widely used. Roxanne Starr Hiltz has undertaken extensive research into the effectiveness of computer conferencing in education in her work with the Virtual Classroom at the New Jersey Institute of Technology. She argues that to be effective, computer conferencing needs to be tightly integrated into the curriculum (Hiltz, 1997). If use of the conferencing facility is not made part of the 'required', graded curriculum, then the majority of the students will not use it. Even those students who do start to use it will quickly conclude that 'there is nothing going on there' and will stop using it. On the other hand, if conferencing is tightly integrated into the teaching programme then this mode of delivery can be as or more effective than more traditional modes of delivery.

One of the major advantages of electronic learning is that it enables students to learn in their own time, at their own pace and in their own location. Print-based distance education offers these advantages as well. However, electronic delivery offers a greater range of presentation options as well as the possibility of tutor–student and student–student interaction. The importance of these advantages will depend on the extent to which an education or training programme is designed to exploit them.

Summary

Learning is concerned with acquiring the capacity to conceptualize and to act appropriately in a particular context. Teaching is about facilitating the acquisition of that capacity. The way in which people act reflects their tacit and explicit knowledge of the situations in which they find themselves from moment to moment. However, a person's tacit and explicit knowledge of a situation will not always give rise to the same response. In that case, people will often act one way when they know they should have 'done something else'. Developing the ability to act appropriately in a particular situation involves engaging in activities which bring one's tacit and explicit knowledge into alignment. This is accomplished through acting in authentic situations.

The knowledge media hold the promise of delivering education and training more effectively by providing students with a much richer environment in which to learn. Whether that promise is realized depends on how the media are used. Thinking of the knowledge media simply in terms of the transmission of information is likely to foster an approach to learning that accentuates the acquisition of explicit knowledge. For the electronic delivery of courses to be effective, it needs to enable learners to engage in associated practice.

However, the delivery of education and training programmes involves much more than simply the delivery of instruction. It also involves the creation of the type of environment in which the full range of academic, administrative and support needs of the learner are met.

Section II: IMPLEMENTATION

Chapter 4

Counting the cost

In this chapter we:

- provide a framework for understanding the cost relationships;
- describe a basic approach for estimating costs;
- examine the question of whether shifting to digital delivery is likely to yield overall cost savings.

Cost differences between resource-based and classroom-based delivery

One of the major reasons why education and training providers show such strong interest in the potential for using the knowledge media in the electronic delivery of courses is the expectation that it will lead to significant cost savings. How realistic is this expectation? To answer that question it is necessary to understand how cost savings are achieved in distance education.

The major factor that influences the costs of delivery of courses is the pedagogical approach, ie whether delivery is resource based or classroom based. Each of these approaches may be applied to the three main delivery modes: on-campus, traditional distance education and electronic delivery. When we use the term 'classroom' in this context, we do not necessarily mean teaching in a physical space; we also include 'remote classroom' and 'virtual classroom' teaching. Table 4.1 shows a breakdown of delivery strategies by mode and approach.

Table 4.1 *Examples of delivery methods employed in resource-based and classroom-based programmes*

Mode	Pedagogical approach	
	Resource-based	**Classroom**
On–campus	Computer-aided learning	Lectures Tutorials Practicals
Traditional off–campus	Print learning package Audiotape Videotape Practical kits	'Remote classroom'
Digital off–campus	Web learning package	Asynchronous learning networks

The two approaches described above exhibit quite different cost structures on account of the investment in the development of resource materials that is required in the case of resource-based learning.

Resource-based delivery involves a different mix of costs from classroom delivery. Whereas in the case of classroom delivery the majority of the costs originate from the salaries of academic staff, in the case of resource-based delivery a significant proportion of the costs originate from the design and development of learning materials that serve as the primary means of instruction and from the maintenance of the specialized infrastructure required for delivery.

Resource-based delivery also involves a different pattern of expenditure from classroom-based delivery. In the case of classroom-based delivery, most costs accrue during the period in which a course is being offered. In the case of resource-based delivery there are large up-front costs which arise from the need to develop courseware and the need to put in place infrastructure for delivery. The courseware development costs need to be apportioned over the life of the materials. For costing purposes it is generally assumed that the life of materials will be five years. However, the actual life of materials is variable and depends on the pace at which a field of study is developing. The infrastructure costs need to be apportioned over the life of the infrastructure components.

It should be pointed out here that there are also quite substantial infrastructure costs associated with classroom delivery in the form of maintenance of grounds and buildings. In the past, the costs associated with these have often not been taken into account. There may be a strong argument for not including capital costs as grounds and buildings usually represent appreciating assets. However, maintenance does represent a real ongoing cost and ought to be taken into account in any comparison.

The scope for cost savings

The potential for obtaining economies of scale through a change in delivery mode depends on whether economies of scale are already being realized. If substantial economies of scale are already being realized, then the scope for achieving additional economies of scale through a change of mode may be small.

If economies of scale are achieved through a shift from classroom-based to resource-based delivery, then the potential for obtaining substantial economies of scale through a shift to electronic delivery is likely to be considerably greater to countries that do not already have a well-developed system of print-based distance education.

The success of the UK Open University led many other countries to establish national open universities based on the Open University model. Examples include the Fernuniversitat in Germany, Sukhothai Thammathirit Open University in Thailand, the Indira Ghandi Open University in India and Athabasca University in Alberta, Canada. The two notable exceptions to this trend have been Australia and the United States.

Australia had a long history of involvement in distance education before the UK Open University was established. It did not follow other countries in setting up a national Open University, but instead it extended its dispersed model in which institutions combined distance teaching with face-to-face teaching. Within these institutions distance education subject enrolments are generally much lower than the enrolments in corresponding subjects in single-mode national distance education providers. Nevertheless, the scale of operations of most Australian distance education providers, together with the lower cost structures of their delivery methods, lets them operate quite efficiently. Their scope for achieving further cost savings by switching to online delivery is therefore limited.

Greatest interest in the potential offered by the World Wide Web and interactive multimedia for lowering the costs of delivery is being shown in the United States. This is only partly explained by the fact that many of the technological developments are originating there. The United States does not have a strong tradition of involvement in distance education. There, participation in distance education has until recently been limited to a small number of providers such as the University of Wisconsin and Penn State University.

The United States did not attempt to establish a national distance education system. However, with the rapid developments in cable and satellite communications technologies in the 1980s, many educational institutions saw the opportunity for entering the field of distance education through the use of audio, audiographic and video conferencing. Consequently, in the United States distance education tends to be conceived of in terms of the 'remote classroom' model.

The great interest being expressed by educational institutions in the United States in the promise of online delivery is therefore partly explained by the fact that the potential for economies of scale has yet to be fully exploited in that country. The possibility for cost savings is consequently much greater. However, the factor that will be responsible for generating the cost savings will the switch from classroom-based to resource-based delivery. The shift to online delivery will merely be the means by which that switch will be accomplished.

The importance of economies of scale

The success of the UK Open University depended on the considerable investment that the university was able to make in the development of learning materials and the implementation of delivery systems. It was able to afford this investment by taking advantage of the potential which exists in resource-based delivery for achieving economies of scale.

Economies of scale can be achieved because of the high proportion of fixed costs to variable costs in resource-based delivery. In classroom delivery, most of the cost of delivery is accounted for by variable costs – that is, costs which vary according to the number of students enrolled. In resource-based delivery, the possibility exists of reducing variable costs by shifting the weight of instruction to packaged learning materials. Reproduction and dispatch of packaged materials is comparatively economical, on a cost per student basis. However, the total cost of development is typically high. Nevertheless, if this cost is spread across a large number of students, the cost per student falls to quite economical levels.

Economies of scale are actually obtainable at two different levels, as Ashenden (1987) showed. At subject level, economies of scale are obtained by spreading the costs of design and development of materials as we have described. However, further economies of scale are obtainable at the institutional level by spreading the fixed capital costs of delivery infrastructure over a growing institutional intake.

The effect of size of intake

It is commonly believed that it is possible to continue to extract worthwhile economies of scale indefinitely with increasing student numbers. This reflects a misconception. The economies of scale that are available through the use of learning packages decline as numbers increase to the point where they are no longer significant. To understand why this is so we need to examine the way in which the costs change with size of intake. The variable we need to look at particularly is the average cost per student of delivering a subject.

Figure 4.1 shows the relationship between the cost per student and the average annual intake for a hypothetical subject involving $50,000 of fixed costs, $250 per student variable costs and a five-year investment recovery period. The actual figures used here are not important. What we are interested in is the trend.

Referring to the figure, it can be seen that with low student numbers, the cost per student of offering a subject is high. Indeed, if numbers are extremely

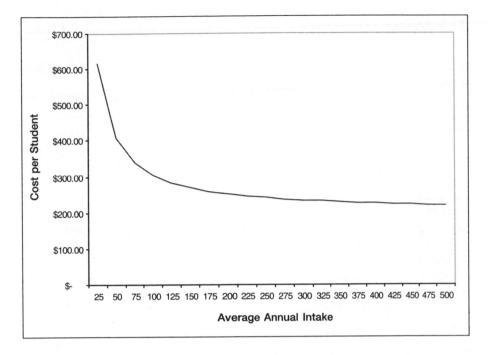

Figure 4.1 *Economies of scale curve*

low – say, less than 10 – the cost per student may be so high that it is uneconomic to offer a subject using typical packaged materials. In that case, one would consider using another delivery strategy or discontinuing the subject.

As the average annual intake rises, the cost per student falls. However, the rate of decline is not constant. Initially, it is quite rapid. Then, as the cost of materials development is spread over a growing number of students, the rate of decline slows. Eventually, the point is reached at which the rate at which the cost per student is falling is so slow that the economies are no longer worth pursuing. Once this point is reached, there is no cost benefit justification for trying to boost the intake further.

Increasing the average annual intake reduces the contribution of fixed costs to the total costs of delivery. As the curve flattens out, it approaches (but never actually reaches) the horizontal straight line representing variable costs per student.

Taking this curve as a starting point, it is easy to see the effect of increasing either the variable or fixed costs. If the variable costs are higher, the curve will have the same shape, but the curve will lie higher up the y-axis. If the fixed costs are higher, then the tail of the curve will extend further to the right. A higher average annual intake will be needed to offer the subject at the same cost per student.

The impact of marketing costs

In a competitive market environment, building and maintaining a market requires investment in marketing and promotion. In highly competitive markets, this represents a significant proportion of the costs of doing business.

Most studies of the costs of distance education have not taken into consideration the costs of marketing. This is because at the time that they were undertaken the demand for places was generally greater than the supply and institutions did not need to market their courses very actively in order to fill their quotas. In any case, the marketing of courses was the responsibility of the central administration and was seldom attributed to individual courses.

As the market for educational programmes became more competitive, institutions began to spend more in this area. Furthermore, teaching departments also began to recognize the importance of actively promoting their own courses. In the devolution of authority, responsibility for marketing of courses was formally handed over to the teaching departments and marketing then appeared as a cost item in their budgets.

If a course is well established and has a strong reputation, the cost of promoting it to prospective students may be relatively small. However, as the market for courses in a particular field approaches saturation, the cost of attracting each additional student rises. Eventually the rate of increase in costs expended on attracting each additional student balances the economic benefit of securing that student. The curve relating marketing costs per student to student intake begins to rise. Consequently, there is a point at which the rising costs of attracting each new student onto a course meets the decrease in delivery costs. At this point there are no further economies of scale to be had. Where this point lies depends to some extent on how well the marketing programme is targeted and therefore how effective it is at reaching potential students.

Thus there will be a point beyond which it will actually be counter-productive to boost intakes. No attempt has been made to allow for the costs of marketing in Figure 4.1 as these are very situation-specific.

The concept of efficiency

Efficiency is concerned with the minimization of the call on resources. If we relate the concept of efficiency to the curve shown in Figure 4.1, we can say that a distance education provider is operating efficiently if all its subjects are operating in the flat part of the curve.

The distinction between efficiency and effectiveness

Effectiveness, in the context of teaching, refers to the extent to which teaching results in changes in a learner's understanding, skills, competencies, attitudes and dispositions.

The aim in education and training is to deliver in ways that are both efficient and effective. However, these goals sometimes compete. The concept of efficiency does not imply effectiveness. While the concept of efficiency implies having the desired effect, it does not imply maximizing effectiveness. The pursuit of efficiency can compromise effectiveness and effectiveness may be pursued at the expense of efficiency. For example, increasing the extent of tutor–student interaction increases the effectiveness with which students learn. However, it also increases the variable costs of provision in relation to fixed costs. The aim is therefore to strike an appropriate balance within the constraints of the available resources.

Taking advantage of economies of scale to manage costs

This highly simplified explanation of the way economies of scale are achieved ignores the many complexities that emerge in the delivery of actual programmes.

In the first place, it doesn't take into consideration the economies of scale that can be obtained at the institutional level. Ashenden (1987) argued that the institutional infrastructure is not used efficiently until the annual student intake across all courses rises above 3,000.

The explanation doesn't take into account, either, the fact that courses typically become more specialized in the later years. Consequently, the number of students enrolled in later-year subjects are usually much lower than the number enrolled in first-year subjects. Annual intakes fall from hundreds or even thousands of students to, in some cases, single-digit figures.

Nevertheless, the explanation does give us sufficient understanding of economies of scale for us to be able to predict, in general terms, the way in which costs will be impacted by changes in delivery mode. If one wishes to drive variable costs down, then the options for achieving this are to eliminate cost components or to make the delivery of these components more efficient.

It can be seen, for example, that making learning packages more self-contained (which reduces students' reliance on tutor and administrator time) will decrease variable costs, thereby increasing the ratio of fixed costs to variable costs and improving the potential for economies of scale. Increasing the extent of student–tutor interaction, on the other hand, will increase variable costs, lower the ratio of fixed costs to variable costs and erode the potential for obtaining economies of scale.

Reducing variable costs has the effect of extending the intake range over which the worthwhile economies of scale can be obtained. Eliminating any of the variable cost components is likely to impact the quality of students' learning and therefore to push up failure and drop-out rates. This approach is sometimes adopted as a short-term expedient to managing funding cuts. However, it carries a longer term cost.

Turoff (1997a) has argued that once a body of subject material is so well understood that it can be delivered via resource materials it is probably not what students of the future will expect of a university education. The approach one adopts to delivering courses needs to take account of the type of learning in which students are or ought to be engaged. In technical and vocational education, the criticism that Turoff has levelled at resource-based learning would not be valid as he himself has acknowledged.

The only way to reduce variable costs without at the same time running the risk of increasing failure and drop-out rates is to improve the efficiency with which services are delivered.

The potential for obtaining economies of scale in online delivery

Because online delivery involves the use of packaged learning materials, the potential exists here too to obtain economies of scale. When online learning is conceived of as the delivery of resource materials via the Internet, the principles that govern the costs of print-based delivery also apply. As in the case of print-based delivery, the magnitude of the economies of scale that can be obtained depends on the ratio of fixed costs to variable costs.

The costs of Web-based development, where it doesn't include interactive multimedia elements, need not be much greater than the costs of print-based development. Indeed, it is technically feasible to develop parallel print- and Web-based versions of a course from the original source material.

If online learning is conceived of as participation in tutor-led asynchronous or synchronous discussions, the ratio of fixed costs to variable costs is low and the opportunities for economies of scale are small to non-existent. Turoff (1997b) has estimated the costs of establishment of a virtual university based on the methods of teaching pioneered at the New Jersey Institute of Technology. He shows that a virtual university could provide tuition at level of cost comparable to those of good face-to-face institutions. However, this result is achieved by balancing an increase in faculty costs against the savings in the costs of buildings and non-faculty staff costs. Turoff argues the case for the virtual university, not in terms of its potential to save costs, but rather in terms of the higher standard of education it would offer students learning at a distance.

Online delivery of courses also offers the opportunity to maximize economies of scale in those courses for which intakes are small by expanding the catchment area from which students are recruited. The cost of delivering to an international market via print is somewhat higher because of the additional mailing and marketing costs. The Internet offers a way of reaching these markets at lower cost. In the case of a course with very low enrolments, this may enable the average annual intake into subjects to be brought to levels where it is possible to deliver the course economically.

What this means in practice is reducing the extent to which students draw on the time of staff – particularly the time of highly-paid staff – for less demanding tasks. Also, there are unlikely to be any savings to be made from switching to online delivery compared with delivering the same materials via print.

The potential for obtaining economies of scale with delivery via interactive multimedia

The cost of development of multimedia materials is typically very much higher than the cost of developing textual materials. A rule of thumb which is often used in estimating the costs of multimedia materials is that it takes of the order of 100 hours of development time to generate one hour of instruction. In order to bring the cost per student of development of multimedia materials down to an acceptable level it is therefore necessary to spread the cost over a very much larger intake than would be the case for print.

The use of interactive multimedia materials therefore implies the need to target a larger student body. Use of interactive multimedia does not generate cost savings in delivery; if anything, it tends to increase costs. The decision to employ interactive multimedia in distance education needs therefore to be justified in terms of the benefits that are offered. The most important benefit that interactive multimedia offers is related to quality of teaching, arising from the capacity of students to visualize processes, to grasp new concepts, to understand processes and procedures – particularly where they involve motion.

We need to be cautious in accepting at face value the claims made for the effectiveness of interactive multimedia. It is clearly incorrect to suggest that the use of interactive multimedia technology *per se* enhances the effectiveness of teaching. Many multimedia productions do little more than present text and graphics on screen. In these cases the multimedia presentation is doing little more than 'page turning'.

One other way in which the use of interactive multimedia materials can be justified in cost-benefit terms is if learning via such materials is much more efficient than learning via textual materials. In this case, using multimedia materials may be able to reduce the time a student needs to spend learning. In a meta-analysis of the results of early research in to the cost efficiency of computer-aided learning, it was shown that such learning took 60 per cent of the time that it took to complete the same course by traditional means.

For the reasons given above, interactive multimedia is best used to target small parts of the curriculum for which it offers a clear advantage. The World Wide Web provides a means of integrating short interactive multimedia segments into learning materials.

If one's objective is to increase the level of investment in the development of learning materials in order to increase their effectiveness, then taking advantage of the potential for achieving economies of scale is the way to do this without impacting overall costs.

Some assumptions upon which the expectation of cost savings is based

The expectation that savings can be made by shifting to electronic delivery is based on a number of assumptions, some of which have not been fully tested.

One of the major assumptions is that the savings in production and mailing costs that can be made by switching from print-based distance education to online distance education will not be fully eroded by costs attributable to the maintenance of the services and infrastructure needed for electronic delivery.

There are a number of new costs that are incurred in moving from print-based to online delivery. These include:

- overhead costs of Web-server and mail-server storage;
- staff costs of Web site maintenance;
- staff costs of registration of students; and
- staff costs of provision of help-desk services.

It is commonly assumed that these costs are negligible. However, analysis of the costs shows them to be quite significant when compared with printing and mailing costs.

However, it appears that the largest cost which is added as a result of moving to online delivery is the cost of communication charges. In Australia, the cost of communication charges will on their own in many cases exceed the cost of printing and dispatch of print-based learning packages. Most institutions anticipate that these costs will be passed on to students. However, this raises issues of equity, which we will return to at the end of this chapter. It also presumes that passing on a significant cost to students will not discourage them from enrolling.

Will shifting to online delivery reduce overall costs?

As indicated in Chapter 2, one of the major reasons why education and training providers are shifting to online delivery is to save costs. However, given what we have said about costs in this chapter, we need to ask whether this expectation is realistic. The answer depends to a considerable extent on the mode or modes of delivery that a provider is presently using.

For universities that have not previously been involved in resource-based learning such a shift offers the possibility of achieving substantial economies of scale just as the shift to print-based distance education has offered in the past. The costs of communication infrastructure can be offset against the cost of buildings that would be required to increase on-campus enrolments to a similar extent. This explains the great interest being shown by US institutions in particular. The lower costs of computer and communications technologies in the United States offer American institutions somewhat lower variable costs. For US institutions involved in synchronous remote classroom delivery, moving to asynchronous online delivery also offers the potential for economies of scale.

However, the situation of US institutions is somewhat different from that of major national distance education providers that have already taken advantage of the economies of scale obtainable from print-based distance education. For these providers the magnitude of the savings will depend on their cost structures and will in most cases be less.

For major Australian distance education providers that are operating highly efficient print-based delivery systems, the shift to online delivery offers little if any prospect of savings. Indeed, the shift may result in significantly increased costs. For these institutions the shift needs to be justified in terms of the educational benefits or the opportunities offered to tap into a more distant market. The challenge for these institutions will not be to realize savings but to manage the transition without escalating costs.

For institutions other than the major national distance education providers the outcome is difficult to predict and will depend on a host of factors including the experience of staff, the size and location of target markets and the nature of the courses offered.

The conclusion to be drawn from this analysis is that the decision to shift to online delivery ought to be made as much on the basis of the educational and marketing advantages to be gained from such a move as on the expectation of savings.

What are the likely costs?

Rumble (1997) pointed out that one of the difficulties that institutions experience in managing the costs of distance education is that line-item budgeting conceals the critical cost relationships. He argues that distance education providers would be better able to manage their budgets if they moved to activity-based costing.

In activity-based costing, the overall delivery costs are subdivided into a number of major activities corresponding to the different phases in the development and delivery process.

It is possible to break down the costs of off-campus delivery into several major categories. These are shown in Figure 4.2. The breakdown is different from that suggested by Rumble, reflecting the just-in-time approach to the reproduction of learning packages more typical of Australian distance education providers. The nomenclature used in the figure has been chosen so as to be applicable across

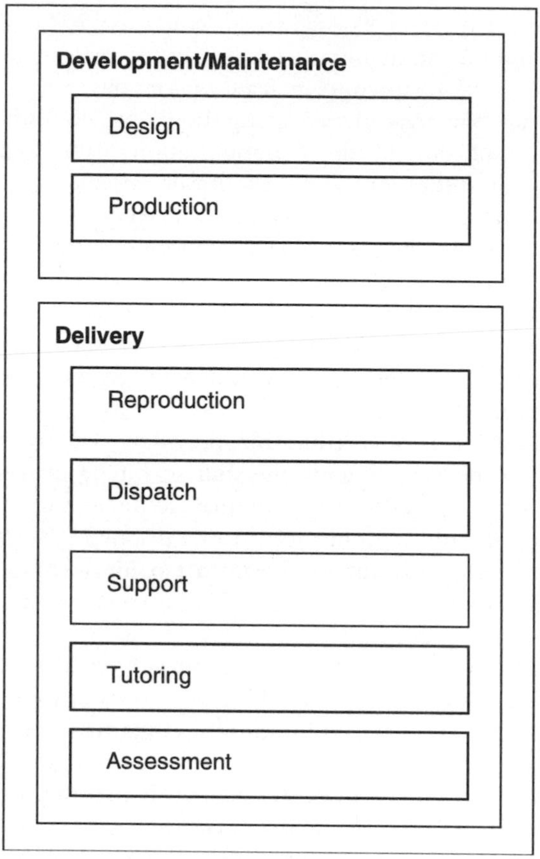

```
┌─────────────────────────────────────────────┐
│  ┌───────────────────────────────────────┐  │
│  │ Development/Maintenance                │  │
│  │  ┌─────────────────────────────────┐  │  │
│  │  │ Design                          │  │  │
│  │  └─────────────────────────────────┘  │  │
│  │  ┌─────────────────────────────────┐  │  │
│  │  │ Production                      │  │  │
│  │  └─────────────────────────────────┘  │  │
│  └───────────────────────────────────────┘  │
│  ┌───────────────────────────────────────┐  │
│  │ Delivery                               │  │
│  │  ┌─────────────────────────────────┐  │  │
│  │  │ Reproduction                    │  │  │
│  │  └─────────────────────────────────┘  │  │
│  │  ┌─────────────────────────────────┐  │  │
│  │  │ Dispatch                        │  │  │
│  │  └─────────────────────────────────┘  │  │
│  │  ┌─────────────────────────────────┐  │  │
│  │  │ Support                         │  │  │
│  │  └─────────────────────────────────┘  │  │
│  │  ┌─────────────────────────────────┐  │  │
│  │  │ Tutoring                        │  │  │
│  │  └─────────────────────────────────┘  │  │
│  │  ┌─────────────────────────────────┐  │  │
│  │  │ Assessment                      │  │  │
│  │  └─────────────────────────────────┘  │  │
│  └───────────────────────────────────────┘  │
└─────────────────────────────────────────────┘
```

Figure 4.2   *Breakdown of activity components*

media. Other terms are in some cases more commonly used with reference to particular media.

While electronic delivery of courses involves the development of quite different resource materials, many of the activities involved in the development of print-based materials are the same or similar. It is therefore possible to draw quite close parallels between the costs of print-based distance education delivery and the costs of online and interactive multimedia delivery.

Table 4.2 shows the activities in Web-based and interactive multimedia delivered via CD ROM against the breakdown that is used in print-based delivery. In the case of interactive multimedia delivered via CD ROM, support, tutoring and the submission and return of assignments will not be specific to this medium.

In using activity-based costing to estimate the costs of a project, the resource requirements of the project are quantified and a total cost is calculated by multiplying each component cost by its corresponding unit cost.

Table 4.2 *Typical activities contributing to activity components*

Activity component	Medium	
	Web	CD ROM
Design	As for print-based delivery	As for print-based delivery
Production	HTML document creation	Storyboarding Scripting Programming
Reproduction	Web site construction	CD ROM duplication
Dispatch	Web site maintenance	Packaging Mailing
Support	Online help-desk Online library services Online counselling	★
Tutoring	Asynchronous conferencing Synchronous conferencing	★
Assessment	★	★

★Typically these components will be provided via alternative media or in other ways.

Table 4.3 identifies the typical cost components for print, Web and interactive multimedia projects. The actual costs of a development project are likely to vary quite widely with an individual provider's situation as well as with the country within which a project is being undertaken. For example, projects that involve a large amount of interactivity and require extensive programming or the creation of sophisticated animations will be much more expensive than projects that provide an interface to a range of existing print, illustration and video resources. Attempting to provide indicative costs for multimedia projects would therefore be more likely to mislead than inform.

If a more sophisticated analysis of the costs of delivering distance education and training via the World Wide Web service is required, then the cost/perform-ance model developed by Bloniarz and Larsen (1997) for the costing of the provision of government information services offers a possible methodology.

Who pays the cost?

In Australia, less than half of all homes have a computer and printer. A far lower proportion have a modem as well. For students who have a computer, printer, modem and access to an Internet account, the marginal cost of using these facilities to access course materials online is likely to be small. However, for students who

Table 4.3 *Cost elements in resource-based learning projects*

Activity component	Cost contributor	Units	Project type		
			Print	Web	CD
Design	Subject specialist	hours	✓	✓	✓
	Teaching-learning specialist	hours	✓	✓	✓
	Multimedia producer	hours			✓
Production	Subject specialist	hours	✓	✓	✓
	Teaching-learning specialist	hours	✓	✓	✓
	Scriptwriter	hours	✓	✓	✓
	Editor	hours			✓
	Cameraman	hours			✓
	Audio producer	hours			✓
	Narrator	hours			✓
	Graphic designer	hours	✓	✓	✓
	Photographer	hours	✓	✓	
	Desktop publisher	hours	✓		
	Web publisher	hours	✓	✓	✓
	Production manager	hours			✓
Reproduction	Printing	pages	✓		
	Binding	volumes	✓		
	Storage	volumes	✓	✓	
	Web database integration	Mbs		✓	
Dispatch	Packaging/postage	packages	✓		✓
	Mail label production	packages	✓		✓
	Stuffing	packages	✓		✓
	Delivery to PO	packages	✓		
	Web delivery	Mbs		✓	
Support	Communications support	students	✓	✓	
	User support	students	✓	✓	
Tutoring	Subject specialist	hours	✓	✓	
Assessment	Examination supervision	centres	✓	✓	✓
	Examiners	students	✓	✓	✓

do not have these facilities, the shift to online learning puts them at considerable disadvantage. These are also likely to be the students who can least afford to acquire them. The shift to online delivery is therefore likely to accentuate educational and social inequalities unless some compensating action is taken.

One way in which it is possible to alleviate this disadvantage is to offer courses in parallel print and online forms. Students are then offered the opportunity to select the form that suits them best. It also avoids the risk that you will lose part of your market during the transitional period.

Summary

Possibly the most important reason why education and training providers are showing such great interest in shifting to delivery via the knowledge media is to lower costs. The way they see this being achieved is by taking advantage of the economies of scale that delivery via these media appears to offer.

The potential for obtaining economies of scale increases with the ratio of fixed costs to variable costs. The major fixed costs include the costs of the infrastructure needed for delivery and the up-front costs of the development of learning packages; the major variable costs include the costs of administration, student support and assessment.

The potential for obtaining economies of scale can be increased by lowering the variable costs. However, this usually means reducing the extent of student–tutor interaction which is generally considered to be detrimental to the quality of the student's learning experience.

The potential for obtaining economies of scale diminishes as the intake into a subject rises above a certain point. Furthermore, in a saturated market, the increase in the cost of boosting intakes is likely to cap the economies of scale that can be achieved.

The potential for obtaining greater economies of scale depends on the current costs of delivery. Economies of scale are generally achieved by replacing classroom-based learning with resource-based learning. Moving from on-campus or 'remote classroom' delivery to delivery via the knowledge media is therefore likely to yield considerable economies of scale. However, switching from print-based delivery to online delivery is unlikely to yield the same savings.

The costs of delivery can be managed more effectively by adopting an activity-based costing approach rather than a line-item approach to budgeting. The costs of Web-based development are comparable to the costs of print-based development. However, the costs of interactive multimedia development are several orders of magnitude higher and are greatly dependent on the nature of the project.

Chapter 5

A cost or an investment?

In this chapter we pose the question: is it more appropriate to regard expenditure on learning materials and delivery system development as an investment rather than simply a cost? We then examine the implications of adopting an investment orientation to the way learning materials and delivery system development is managed. We examine in particular the implications for:

- protection of intellectual property;
- returns on the investment;
- responding to competition.

We conclude by discussing the importance of being able to monitor the real costs of development and maintenance.

The importance of seeing learning materials and delivery systems as assets

In the last chapter we explained that the costs of mounting a distance education programme can be divided into up-front expenses and on-going expenses. The up-front expenses include the cost of design, development and pre-production of materials as well as the cost of establishing the infrastructure needed to support the on-going delivery of programmes. Providers of traditional print-based distance education programmes have tended to treat these expenses merely as costs. The literature examining the economics of distance education has also generally dealt with them in this way. Yet in other industries they would be treated as investments.

The way one thinks about an expenditure affects the way one manages it. The tendency to regard the expenditure on development of courseware simply as a cost is one of the main factors that in the past has discouraged many tertiary education institutions from entering the field of distance education. The high up-front costs of development were seen as a barrier to entry into distance education. Institutions could not see the justification for incurring such large costs when they were not incurred on programmes entirely taught within an annual budget period.

However, learning materials have a value that survives for several years. This value subsists both in the materials themselves and also in the knowledge derived from the research that went into their development. This knowledge may be drawn on again for the production of materials in a different form. The learning materials should therefore be regarded as assets. Correspondingly, the expense of developing the learning resource materials should be seen as an investment rather than simply a cost. The same reasoning can also be applied to the expenditure on new delivery systems.

What difference does it make to treat an expense as an investment?

In the commercial world, the profitability of a company depends on the return it makes on its assets. In the public sector, the health of an organization depends on the income it is able to generate from use of its assets. The financial viability of an organization depends on the success it has in building up and protecting its assets.

In the past, distance education providers often did not display the same concern for their investment in courseware and delivery systems as a manufacturer does for its assets in product designs and manufacturing plant and equipment. One of the first differences concerns the way in which decisions are made as to how much to spend on courseware development. A manufacturer will spend whatever is needed to produce and market a product that meets the expectation of the market being targeted. Distance education providers, on the other hand, will often try to keep costs to a minimum even when that means lowering the quality of the product. This approach may be tenable in a captive market. However, in a competitive market, the quality of the product is of paramount importance. Investing too little on initial development may result in a product that is unable to return its initial investment.

Once a product has been launched efforts will be made to preserve the value of the resulting asset. The types of action include:

- protecting the intellectual property which gives the product its uniqueness in the market;
- ensuring that the return on the investment is maximized by marketing the product appropriately and adequately;
- ensuring that the appearance of the product is not allowed to become tired and outdated, by regularly updating it.

Making the investment decision

While it is a mistake to spend too little on the development of a new course, it is obviously also a mistake to spend too much or to invest in a course for which there is insufficient demand.

Yet how should you decide what is an adequate return? The answer will depend on the nature of the project.

A general rule that is applied within the investment community is that the rate of return one should look for from an investment should reflect the level of risk being taken. If one applies this rule to the provision of distance education offerings, then when investing in the development of courses which do not have a guaranteed intake one should be looking for a higher return than in developing courses which do have a guaranteed intake. However, it is only prudent to accept a higher level of risk if this risk is spread across a larger number of projects. This allows losses on loss-making projects to be set against the higher returns on profit-making projects. Nevertheless, irrespective of the element of risk involved, the greater the margin the more attractive will be the project.

The factor that most determines where best to seek a market is the margin you can achieve between the unit cost of supply and the revenue you can obtain. The greater the margin the more attractive the investment opportunity. However, profits can still be made by achieving small margins per unit on products that achieve high sales figures.

In the case of government-funded courses, budgeting is directed towards producing the best result with the funds provided. There is no call to achieve a surplus and the funds available are often less than one would ideally like to commit.

The situation can be different for full-fee courses offered by government-funded institutions. In this case it may be expected that the conduct of courses will generate a surplus to provide for growth or to support other activities in which the institution is engaged. In this case, the cost of offering the course needs to be looked at against the potential income. Some projects may be worth undertaking because of the size of the market. Other projects will be attractive because they offer the prospect of better than average margins.

The factors that are critical to making a good investment decision are:

- you have adequate knowledge of the particular market;
- you have a good understanding of what your costs will be in entering that market.

The most common mistakes are to overestimate the size of the market for a particular product and to underestimate the costs of development. It is therefore advisable to allow for a wide margin of error in making your estimates.

Planning for the investment

Making the transition to delivery via the knowledge media involves a major investment in the development of new courseware. It also requires substantial infrastructure investment – in upgrading communications networks, acquiring and installing new server hardware and acquiring software licences. There is also a substantial investment in training staff.

Making the right investment decisions calls for the development of a plan as a basis for first deciding whether it is prudent to proceed in the form originally proposed, or whether the proposal needs modification. This plan may take a form similar to that of a business plan which is drawn up for starting a new venture. The plan should detail the scope of the changes proposed, the sequence in which it is proposed they be undertaken, the projected costs and the return that is expected set out on a year-by-year basis for a three to five-year period.

Such a plan should be drawn up before your entry into a new media programme, including cases where you are shifting from print based to electronic delivery. However, a smaller scale plan ought to be drawn up prior to making an investment in any new course area. An approach that may be used in the development of a plan is described in Chapter 11.

The most important part of the plan is the financial information. This needs to detail not just the costs that will be involved, but also the expected return on the investment. Return on investment may be derived from several income streams. For example, in addition to enrolling students, some or all of the courseware may be sold as a product on its own. In addition, the rights to use some of the courseware in another course may be sold to another education and training provider. Even if no money is to change hands, a notional estimate of income and expenditure should be prepared as part of the justification for the project in order to check that the project will justify committing the resources that will be needed.

Protecting the intellectual property component of courseware

The intellectual property of courseware is protected through copyright. Copyright is intended to allow originators of works to obtain adequate reward for their efforts. Copyright protects the expression of the work, not the ideas that led to the creation of the work.

Copyright legislation differs from country to country. It is therefore important for you to be conversant with the copyright law that applies in your country and to be aware of the extent of the protection that the law gives to the materials that you are producing.

The intellectual property which subsists in courseware has hitherto been more closely related to the subject matter content than to the pedagogical structure of the courseware. The frequency with which courseware needs to be updated is determined more by changes in the currency of subject matter than by the pedagogical approach. Pedagogy is not advancing as rapidly as the majority of other fields of study, although there are nevertheless significant opportunities for innovation in the way a course is offered, through applying the results of educational research. However, copyright subsists in the expression of ideas and multimedia products offer much more opportunity for individual expression than print-based materials have in the past.

In Chapter 7, we will discuss the option of outsourcing the development of courseware. Outsourcing the programming of multimedia courseware or the design of a Web site may enable you to shorten the development cycle for a project. However, it is important to establish what rights you are receiving to the courseware or Web pages. If you employ contractors under standard terms then what you may be paying for is the right to use the courseware or Web pages rather than the copyright over the materials themselves. This will mean that you won't have the right to alter the material in future except by employing the same contractor. If you wish to retain the copyright over the materials, then you may need to make explicit provision in the contract you sign with the contractor.

Even if you do have a contract that gives copyright in the materials to your organization, this only protects the materials. Copying a CD ROM without the permission of the copyright owner is a breach of the copyright law. However, adapting the ideas that have been used in producing the CD ROM to produce another product that looks quite different is not a breach of copyright. Indeed, this is one of the most common ways in which ideas for new products arise.

It is important to realize that consultants make a living by selling the skills they pick up in moving from job to job. Commercial-in-confidence conditions are difficult to define and to enforce. If the project for which you are employing the contractors is to implement a smart new way of presenting a multimedia package, then it may not be too many months before your competitors are also using this approach. Obtaining compensation for breaches of agreement may be difficult and is almost certain to take considerable time.

In commerce, most innovation is actually adaptation of ideas. In manufacturing industries, many companies rely on rapid innovation to keep one step ahead of their competitors. One way of dealing with the matter of copyright is therefore to aim to be providing the most up-to-date instruction and to be known for that.

Maximizing the return on assets

One of the most commonly given reasons for wanting to move to digital delivery is that it opens up a much wider market. It extends existing markets by allowing students to enrol who hitherto have been unable to attend on-campus classes because of work and other commitments. It also opens the door to new more geographically distant markets. Yet the fact that you may gain access to a much larger market does not guarantee that you will be able to tap that market successfully. The strategies that you have found most successful in the past may simply not be appropriate to the new media. Even if they are appropriate they may not be effective.

At a time when everyone is scrambling their way up a steep learning curve, there are few hard and fast rules. Perhaps the best advice that can be given is to keep trying new ideas. Stay with those strategies that produce results and discard those that prove ineffective. To avoid repetition of failed ventures and to make best use of successful tactics it is important to keep a record of your results; to systematize the construction and maintenance of corporate memory.

To come up with new ideas, put yourself in the shoes of the customers you are hoping to attract. If you were one of them, how would you be likely to learn what courses are available?

If you plan to use the Internet, be aware that the major search engines locate sites that are frequently changing. Sites that stagnate disappear from view. So, by continuing to improve and expand your site you can increase its prominence.

Be selective in how you advertise. Internet users are becoming chary of advertisers who fill Usenet newsgroups with advertisement and their mailboxes with unsolicited mail.

Keeping courseware current

Maintaining an investment, like maintaining a home, requires ongoing expenditure. It is necessary to budget for this. The cost of marketing, evaluation and updating of courseware and systems should be budgeted on a year-by-year basis. While this might seem like an optional expense, failing to allow for it will eventually affect the competitiveness of your products and show up on the 'bottom line'. As in the case of owning a home, regular maintenance generally ends up costing less than major reconstruction necessitated by neglect.

The fact that courseware can so easily be reproduced makes it tempting to continue using it even when it is out of date. Yet failure to maintain the currency of learning packages can cost real money, not just a provider's reputation.

As students bear an increasing proportion of the cost of their education, they are likely to become more discriminating in what they regard as acceptable quality. In a competitive environment, providers that are able to claim that they are offering the most up-to-date training are likely to attract a larger clientele.

Regular revision of courseware involves significant additional expense. If this task is to be assured of receiving adequate attention, specific budget provision needs to be made for it. Budget provision should also be made for conducting the evaluations which should inform the revisions (see Chapter 10).

Keeping systems up to date

If you commit substantial funds to courseware maintenance, then it represents poor economy to allow the support system needed for course delivery to slide into obsolescence through failing to provide sufficient funds for its maintenance also. It is not uncommon for educational institutions to adopt the attitude, 'If it ain't broke don't fix it.' Commercial providers are generally more aware of the hidden costs of outdated and inefficient support systems, probably because their attention is focused more closely on the 'bottom line'. Yet systems that have been in use for several years without ever having been reviewed become inefficient as well as a barrier to innovation.

Support systems should streamline delivery processes rather than determine them. The design of support systems should be determined by educational rather than engineering criteria. It is nevertheless important for reliability and maintainability that appropriate standards of software and hardware design are still met. The maintenance of support systems therefore demands close cooperation between staff involved in the educational design and those involved with the maintenance of course support systems.

Regular maintenance of support systems will also require a budget allocation. A strategy that may be worthwhile considering is to make specific provision each year for the updating of systems and to apply this to the tasks that have highest priority. In this way it is possible to maintain a priority list of tasks needing attention in the safe knowledge that at least the most important tasks will receive some attention.

Responding to competition

As well as offering access to new markets, the Internet exposes providers to much greater competition. The effect of competition is to drive prices (in this case course fees) lower. If competition becomes so intense that revenue falls below the cost of getting the product to market, some suppliers are driven out of the market. This eases pressure on prices and leads to an equilibrium being established where prices are sufficient to allow a profit margin which is acceptable to at least a few suppliers. The suppliers that still remain in the market once this stage has been reached will be those that operate most efficiently.

In a global market for online courses, we should therefore expect that survival will depend on efficiency of provision rather than just price. As was shown in the previous chapter, except where a very substantial investment has been made in development, the size of intake needed to reach efficiency is actually quite modest. You could decide that rather than go head-to-head in a global market for online provision of the most popular courses, you will seek out niche markets where there is under-provision. Meeting a need in an area where there is high demand and insufficient supply allows a greater return.

Institutions that do well will be those that are able to spot new opportunities and are nimble at meeting those opportunities. This is the essence of an investment approach to course provision.

Our intention here has not been to provide a comprehensive treatment of all the factors that need to be taken into account in adopting an investment orientation to entering the online education market. Rather, it has been to highlight the changes in ways of thinking about course development and course delivery that the adoption of an investment approach implies.

The importance of real-cost accounting

Moving to online delivery will involve major budget adjustments. The changes may have important implications for the distribution of powers and responsibilities within an institution. Making such adjustments entails significant risks because the effects of the adjustments cannot be fully known in advance. Unforeseen expenses may arise. However, the risks are greatly magnified if the data upon which the effects of the adjustments are assessed do not reflect the effect of the changes on the organization's overall financial position.

The reason for not using true-cost accounting in transferring expenses between sections is usually to encourage particular behaviour. The effect of pricing services at less than their true cost is for the organization as a whole to subsidize the users of certain services. However, one effect of using internal transfer pricing to do this is to reduce the ability of the organization to monitor the financial impact of resource utilization decisions. This makes it difficult to monitor the results of strategic decisions. A better way to encourage change is through explicit specific-purpose subsidies.

The adoption of real-cost accounting practices enables strategic decisions to be made based on the real cost to the organization of those decisions.

Summary

Treating the initial expenditure on courseware and delivery systems development as an investment implies looking for a return which justifies the magnitude of the expenditure. The initial investment needs to be sufficient to allow products to be developed that meet the current expectations of the education and training market-place. Yet it is equally important not to rush into investment that is never likely to be recovered.

Once funds have been committed, it is important to preserve and enhance the value of the assets that are acquired. As a result:

- delivery systems need to be kept operating efficiently;
- courseware needs to be kept current in terms of its content, teaching effectiveness and appearance;
- opportunities need to be sought for deriving additional returns through exploiting courseware and delivery systems.

Chapter 6

Re-engineering technological infrastructure

In this chapter we will examine the changes to information technology infra-structure that a major shift to online or multimedia delivery will necessitate. We examine three options for implementing an integrated electronic learning environ-ment and describe a number of commercially-available products that perform this role. We also identify the types of changes that will need to be made to communications infrastructure and discuss the vexed issue of access.

The importance of setting a target

Undertaking a major shift to delivery online or via multimedia almost invariably requires a major investment in upgrading information technology infrastructure. Servers to hold and deliver will need to be installed, networks will need to be upgraded to carry the much greater traffic resulting from the transmission of graphics, audio and video files, licences for courseware authoring tools will need to be acquired, and software systems will need to be implemented to manage the many transactions between student and provider that henceforth will be mediated by computer.

The scale and nature of the changes that will be required will depend first and foremost on how great a shift is being envisaged. The initial investment that you will need to make is likely to be substantial. You therefore need to be confident that the changes you make are appropriate and will leave you well-placed for moving forward in the future.

Laying the appropriate foundations for future developments depends on carefully thinking through the types of activities in which you plan to be engaged. You need to ask:

- Are you intending to move only into multimedia development (ie, distributing courseware on CD ROM) or are you intending to deliver courses online?
- Are you intending to offer parallel versions of courses via print and online?
- If you are intending to deliver courses online, do you want to start to include interactive multimedia resources in your Web pages or are you willing to limit the contents of pages to print and simple illustrations initially?

The general trend among distance education providers is now towards delivering courseware via the Web rather than via CD ROM. The convergence of technologies is now enabling interactive multimedia to be delivered online. Not only can audio and video be delivered across the Internet in real time using software such as Quicktime, Real Audio and Real Video, but users of authoring systems such as Director and Toolbook are being provided with the tools to enable courseware written in these systems also to be delivered online. Nevertheless, setting up your server facilities and providing students with the tools to access Web-based interactive multimedia still involves some preparation, and the quality of reproduction that is possible is greatly inferior to that which is obtained from a video cassette recorder.

If you are intending to start by delivering multimedia courseware on CD ROM then your requirements will be much more modest. Most computers are now sold with CD ROM drives built-in. By paying attention to the selection of software required for replay, it is possible to produce CD ROMs that are platform independent.

The main components of a delivery system

In Chapter 3 we outlined the basic functions that need to be supported in an electronic learning environment. Most multimedia authoring systems are essentially designed as presentation tools. The need to be able to develop complete courses online has led to the development of a new generation of course delivery systems which don't as yet have a generally recognized name but which we will refer to as 'integrated electronic learning environments'. Such systems combine a range of functions including courseware presentation, test administration and conferencing, and a unified user interface. However, it is also possible to develop an electronic learning environment by bringing together a range of components from different suppliers. The development of the World Wide Web has made the task of combining the use of such systems much simpler than it would have been in the past. Each of the otherwise separate components can be linked to a common Web page. In many cases even the design of the interface to components can be customized so that they display a provider's logo rather than the banner for the software product.

Once you have set up your delivery system you will still need to provide the courseware that provides the primary instruction. If you are intending to deliver courses over the Web and initially limit the style of courseware you provide to text and illustrations, then a wide range of options are available for the creation of Web pages. Most current word processing and desktop publishing systems offer the capability of outputting text in HTML format as is needed for publishing on the Web. This approach will be quite satisfactory. However, if you are intending to develop Web courseware that makes extensive use of illustrations and a complex hyperlinked structure then you will find it beneficial to re-examine all the processes involved in courseware development. Most software developers are marketing tools that are more suited to the development of Web-based illustrations and text than the tools designed for print publishing. For example, Macromedia, now one of the leading suppliers of Web authoring tools, has developed separate products for creation of Web graphics and Web animations. One of the important ways in which tools intended for Web page design differ from those meant for print publishing is that they make much more economical use of storage capacity and as a consequence make much more economical use of bandwidth.

If you are intending to go further and develop multimedia resources then you will need to acquire licences for the authoring software and other development tools. If you are intending to deliver multimedia courseware over the Web, then you may require additional software to enable your server to support this function.

Finally, if the equipment that your staff are currently using is somewhat dated, then you may need to consider upgrading or replacing it. In any case, you should start to put in place an ongoing programme for equipment replacement. When the delivery of education and training programmes begins to rely on the computers then it is no longer satisfactory to wait to replace computers until they are uneconomical to repair. The factor that should decide whether computers are due for replacement is whether they can perform the functions they need to economically.

The major components of development and delivery infrastructure that you will need to consider re-engineering will include computer and communications hardware and software to support development and delivery. To be more specific, it will include:

- management systems needed to deliver courses online;
- authoring software for multimedia courseware development;
- computer hardware for courseware development.

An integrated electronic learning environment

Education and training providers that only offer courses taught face-to-face generally have some type of student records system to manage the information they need to keep on their students. This information mainly relates to assigning students to classes, fee collection and student accreditation. To enable students to gain the full benefits of interactive multimedia, it is necessary to maintain at least some record of students' interactions with the courseware.

Integrated electronic learning environments incorporate:

- learning management facilities including online registration, user authentication, online assessment on demand, progress monitoring and reporting for individuals, groups and course material usage, the capacity to update content and preferably the ability to modify course content for the individual student;
- a bank or a directory of learning resources;
- collaborative facilities including file sharing and shared working space, preferably with application sharing and shared virtual whiteboard facilities;
- messaging systems including one-to-one, one-to-many and many-to-many, preferably with the many-to-many feature available synchronously.

The learning management facility, as the name suggests, manages the student's learning programme. The functions of such a system include:

- registering and authenticating users;
- distributing course information, including:
   learning objectives,
   information on learning activities,
   details of other learning resources;
- distributing courseware including multimedia courseware;
- providing information on other learning opportunities such as:
   broadcasts,
   audio, video and computer conferences;
- administering tests and assessments;
- directing the pathways taken by students through courses on the basis of their results on tests and other assessments;
- maintaining records of students' progress;
- providing statistical information on:
   student progress,
   test item analyses,
   materials usage.

Actual integrated learning applications may not exhibit all these features but some come close.

The metaphors matter. The staff development challenge for education and training providers is to generalize the change to new learning technologies from the initial innovators and enthusiasts to the early adopters and from there to the rest of the field. Studies of change indicate that the process is often difficult to carry through. The metaphors associated with integrated learning packages assist the everyday teacher to associate the capabilities of the software with familiar teaching tasks and challenges.

Education and training providers that deliver by distance education need to keep track of a much larger amount of information. Not only is it necessary to keep a record of students' academic progress, it is also necessary to 'track' what has been sent out to students and what students have, in turn, sent back. Distance education tracking systems differ from student records systems in that they follow a student's progress within a subject. They therefore operate at a lower level than student records systems and are generally designed as separate information management systems. Most of the transactions will have nothing to do with the functions of the student records system. However, a distance education database needs to be able to link up with its corresponding student records database in order to download enrolment details at the start of an offer period and perhaps to upload students' results at the end.

Moving to online delivery results in a further increase in the volume and complexity of the information that needs to be managed. To begin with, a great deal more information needs to be held on each student. For example, it is necessary to store information on students' access rights to computer facilities and courseware. It is also necessary to store information on students' learning. This information may range from responses to computer-marked tests to records of the pathway that students have taken through a subject.

Curriculum models

The type of information management system needed to track students' progress through a course depends on the type of delivery model being adopted.

In traditional distance education programmes, courses are divided into subjects. Depending on the type of programme, students may either be required to follow a set course of study or may be able to put together their own course of study by selecting from a 'smorgasbord' of subjects.

In traditional programmes, subjects are divided into sections based on topics and subtopics. The traditional distance education courses therefore follow a model centred on the subject matter to be covered.

In technical and vocational education there has recently been a strong move away from the subject-matter-oriented model towards a model centred on the competencies that students are expected to attain.

The type of curriculum model adopted affects the approach taken towards both assessment and course delivery. In a programme designed according to the subject-matter-oriented model a student satisfies the requirements for receiving an award by completing the assessment set down for each subject. In a programme designed according to the competency-oriented model a student satisfies the requirements for an award by attaining the specified competencies. In the traditional delivery model, delivery of programmes is centred on delivery of the learning materials. The adequacy of these materials is judged according to how well they cover the subject matter of the course. In the competency-based model delivery of programmes is centred on the certification of competencies.

These basic differences between the subject-matter-oriented model and the competency-oriented model have important consequences for the type of information that needs to be held by a learning management system.

Tailoring a learning management system to the curriculum model

A learning management system designed to support courses based on a subject matter award structure will be oriented to recording the key progress information associated with the completion of subjects. It will key sets of test items to the topics into which the subject matter has been divided.

A learning management system designed to support an award structure based on attainment of specified competencies will be oriented to tracking students' attainment of those competencies.

The problem that arises in characterizing programmes according to these two models is that many providers are using either a combination of both models or a hybrid of the two. This will especially be the case for dual sector (higher education/vocational education) public sector institutions. Existing learning management systems are generally designed to support the subject model. It is technically feasible to design a learning management system that could support both models.

Alternative approaches to acquiring an online learning management system

There are three general approaches that one may take to acquiring a learning management system:

- custom designing from the ground up;
- purchasing a system 'off the shelf';
- assembling a system from commercially available 'building blocks'.

The 'custom design' option

Adopting the custom design option will give you a system that is fully tailored to your needs – provided that you can afford the cost of development. If you have the resources, this strategy can offer a competitive advantage insofar as it enables you to incorporate exactly the combination of features you require and to continue to develop the system in directions and at a pace that matches your strategic plans. It will also give you a system which is capable of being enhanced as your needs change, for example when you want to introduce an innovation in the way your delivery system operates.

The major disadvantages of the custom design option are the cost and the work involved in obtaining what is wanted. The time taken to develop such a system is also considerable. Meanwhile the field is advancing apace. For these reasons, custom designing a learning management system is usually an option only for the very largest providers and then only for providers that are in a position to assign a team of software developers to the task full time.

The 'off-the-shelf' option

The number of commercially available learning management systems is growing rapidly. They range from systems suitable for a few hundred students to several thousands.

Some of the advantages of choosing the 'off-the-shelf' option are that the software developer has addressed all of the issues of research, system architecture, programming and trialing. Maintenance and updating are also taken care of by the software developer.

Examples of commercially available integrated learning environments include Learning Space developed by Lotus Corporation; WebCT developed by the Department of Computer Science at the University of British Columbia, which offers more individualized than collaborative features; Toolbook II, which is essentially a multimedia authoring program, but which, in conjunction with Librarian, provides a distribution and learning management system; and The Learning Manager developed by Campus America, which has a strong learning management system and may be used with WebBoard for online messaging.

This is likely to be the approach that suits most providers because it allows a learning management system to be implemented quickly and at minimum risk. However, choosing an off-the-shelf system eliminates one possible source of competitive advantage. A trend that is evident among suppliers of commercially available integrated learning management systems is to allow those parts of the system that the user sees – the interfaces – to be customized. Providers may be able to incorporate their own logo, to design their own icons and to rearrange the menus and other interface components.

The 'building block' option

The building block option offers an incremental strategy.

While off-the-shelf systems may allow a modest amount of customization, a much greater amount is possible when the building block approach is adopted. In this case, the system is assembled from a set of major functional components, each of which is a commercially available product. For example, the conferencing component may be provided by one supplier, the Web server may be provided by a second supplier, and the testing system by a third. The total suite of software may comprise more than half a dozen individual products.

The building block approach is made feasible by the fact that it is now possible to conceal the functional components of a system behind an interface based on Web pages. Users interact with the different components by means of controls which have the same 'look and feel'.

The building block option offers the advantages, while avoiding some of the disadvantages, of the 'off-the-shelf' approach. Each of the components of a system assembled using this approach is a commercially available, fully maintained product. However, the system as a whole can be tailored to the needs of the delivery model.

The main disadvantage of the building block approach is that one has to deal with a number of suppliers rather than just one. This requires a greater investment in management of the system. It will also requires an additional investment in assembling the various components and ensuring they work together. (However, incompatibility of systems is not likely to be a major problem because the various systems still function more or less independently.)

The building block approach is a cost-effective solution to providers that want to obtain a competitive advantage by offering a unique combination of delivery options tailored to the specific needs of their target client group. However, in order to pursue this option a provider will need to have staff to manage the implementation, maintenance and upgrading of the system. Without such support, it is unlikely that the advantages of adopting the approach will be realized and the provider may experience ongoing operational problems.

Some 'off-the-shelf' integrated electronic learning environments

Because of the number of integrated electronic learning environments that are now on the market it is not practicable to provide a comprehensive, up-to-date catalogue of such systems in a book like this. Indeed, given the pace at which the market is growing, any such catalogue would soon be out of date. Nevertheless, it is important to be aware of the types of systems available and the types of functions that they support. We shall therefore briefly describe five of the most popular:

- FirstClass Collaborative Classroom;
- Learning Space;
- The Learning Manager;
- TopClass;
- WebCT.

All of these systems with the exception of the last have been available for some time. However, each has a different heritage, which is reflected in the combination of features it offers.

FirstClass Collaborative Classroom

Latest version: 1.0
<http://www.education.softarc.com/index.html>
FirstClass began as an e-mail and conferencing system designed specifically to meet the needs of education. It is marketed by SoftArc Inc. FirstClass has been

used extensively by the UK Open University. FirstClass Collaborative Classroom incorporates Intranet and Internet access including the ability to publish HTML documents.

One of the major strengths of FirstClass has always been its ability to run on a range of server types and support a range of client types, including Macintosh, Windows, DOS and Unix.

As with other groupware products that have been migrated to the Web, FirstClass lost some of the functions that the client-server version offered. SoftArc is moving to restore these functions by the development of JAVA client applets. FirstClass does not yet offer many of the features of a fully integrated learning environment. It does not offer any learning management features; nor does it offer any testing grade reporting functions. The major strengths of FirstClass Collaborative Classroom are its support for collaborative learning and its cross-platform capabilities.

Learning Space

Latest version: 2.5
<http://www.lotus.com/home.nsf/tabs/learnspace>
Learning Space has been built on top of the groupware product Lotus Notes and the Domino Web server software. Lotus Notes is considered the leading groupware product for business and Learning Space takes advantage of the features Lotus Notes offers for conferencing, e-mail and scheduling. However, Learning Space is not just a groupware product. It is also designed to provide access to a wide range of Web-based interactive multimedia courseware and to support online testing.

Learning Space comprises five distinct databases:

1. Schedule – directs students through a course;
2. Media Centre – for distribution of courseware;
3. Course Room – a discussion area;
4. Profiles – provides information on students;
5. Assessment Manager – supports administration of tests.

Learning Space also provides a range of tools to assist instructors in courseware development, administration and learning management.

Lotus Corporation was taken over by IBM some years ago and so Learning Space is effectively IBM's version of an electronic learning environment.

Learning Space may be accessed via a Lotus Notes Windows, Macintosh or OS/2 client or via a Web browser. It is supported on Unix, Windows NT, Windows 98 and OS/2 servers.

The Learning Manager

Latest version: 2.0

<http://www.campuscan.com/>

The Learning Manager (TLM) has evolved from The Learning Management System (LMS) one of the leading computer-managed learning systems. LMS was developed at the Southern Alberta Institute of Technology (SAIT) and was subsequently acquired by Campus America. LMS was one of the earliest CML systems. However, it was designed to run under Digital's VMS operating system as a distributed, text-based system. In time it was overtaken by microcomputer-based CML and CAL systems that offered graphical user interfaces. TLM is a microcomputer-based system that has been derived from LMS.

TLM differs from LMS in that it is able to run either on individual workstations or over the Internet. When it is used over the Internet it is accessed via a standard Web browser. In this mode it is not platform specific. However, assembly of courseware must be completed on a workstation running under Windows.

Because of its CML origins, TLM possess all the attributes of a true learning management system. In directs the pathway the student takes through a course based on the student's performance on computer-administered tests. The tests use items randomly selected from sets in a test item bank. The system can support a wide range of item types.

The Web compliant version of TLM is paired with WebBoard and WebSite by O'Reilly Software to produce a full integrated electronic learning environment. TLM, WebBoard and WebSite all run under Windows NT.

The major strengths of TLM remain its wide range of learning management and test administration capabilities.

TopClass

Latest version: 2.0

<http://www.wbtsystems.com/index.html>

TopClass was originally marketed as WEST. It is produced by WBT Systems in Ireland. It offers built-in messaging and conferencing facilities.

TopClass is capable of importing and exporting course content in a wide range of formats. The sequences that students follow in taking a course delivered via TopClass can be individually tailored according to their performance on tests administered by the system. A course can be personalized to the individual student to allow relevant and effective learning. The system also provides an extensive range of tracking and reporting tools. TopClass therefore combines the features of a computer-managed learning system, a groupware system and a courseware delivery system.

All users access the system via any browser which supports forms and tables. TopClass runs under various versions of Unix, Windows NT or Windows 98, and Mac OS.

WebCT

Latest version: 1.2
<http://homebrew.cs.ubc.ca/webct/webct.html>
Unlike the preceding products in this list, WebCT was not initially developed with the intention that it be marketed commercially. It has been developed by the Department of Computer Science at the University of British Columbia and was originally intended to support the department's own online programs. However, interest in the system was so great that the University licensed the system to other organizations. Much of the initial development effort was supported by research grants. Income for licence fees is now being used for further continuing development as the initial grants have run out.

Notwithstanding its origins, WebCT is a robust product offering a variety of features including a conferencing system, online chat, tracking of student progress, organization of group projects, student self-assessment, maintenance and publishing of grades, automatic index generation, course content searches, a course calendar and student home pages.

All users of WebCT including course developers, students and markers, access the system via a standard Web browser. The system currently runs under various versions of Unix. An NT version is being developed.

Which system should you choose?

The integrated electronic learning environments described above are only some of a growing array of products being marketed commercially. No doubt new products will be released even before this book is published. If you have decided to opt for a commercially-available system and have reached the stage of making a selection you will need to do your own review of the range of products currently available and the features they offer. Different universities are regularly putting comparisons of the most popular products on their Web sites. Computer magazines and some journals in the field of educational technology also publish reviews from time to time. Most system developers have Web sites advertising their products and these generally give technical details of the features offered.

Having collected the most up-to-date information on the most likely contenders, you are still faced with the task of making the selection decision. This is not as straightforward as determining which product offers most features. To begin with, many systems are only available for certain platforms.

There is a widely-held view in information technology that the selection of software should precede the selection of hardware. In other words, users should choose the software that best suits their application and then choose the hardware that is required to run it. Of course, many software packages run on more than one platform. That situation can simplify as well as complicate the selection decision.

If this principle is applied to the selection of an electronic learning environment, then the first decision that needs to be made concerns the electronic learning environment that best matches the delivery model you intend to employ. Are you intending to base your model mainly on group interaction? If so, you will want a learning environment that supports electronic person-to-person communication. Are you intending to make extensive use of computer-supplied feedback? In this case you will need an electronic learning environment which provides a good range of test administration features. Ideally, it should also provide facilities for test item analysis.

An important feature that providers that maintain their own administrative systems may need is the ability to access the database that holds student and course information. If you are likely to want to transfer student or course data to and from other systems then you will want a system that is open rather than one that requires you to transfer data through a proprietary interface. A checklist of features to look for in integrated electronic learning environments is given in Table 6.1.

Finally, one of the most important considerations ought to be cost. Depending on the number of learners you will be supporting, the cost of acquiring a licence for an electronic learning environment can be quite substantial. Fortunately the licence fees are generally on a sliding scale based on the number of users. In some cases, as for example is the case for WebCT, the cost per user drops as the number of users rises.

Solving the problem of access

Distance educators have been wrestling with the problem of finding ways to give students network access for almost 20 years. The solutions that they have come up with have varied as technology has evolved. The Australian experience in this area has probably not differed greatly from the experience in other Western countries.

Institutions first began providing remote access to computer facilities when they began teaching computing subjects at a distance. At this early stage of development, access was provided via dial-in connections. Students were required to use a modem and telephone line. If the student was located a long distance from an institution then this was expensive and sometimes unreliable.

As the number of institutions providing dial-in access grew and permanent data connections were established between institutions, cooperative arrangements were entered into to enable students to reach the institution at which they were enrolled by dialling-in to a local institution and then connecting across the network. The establishment of the Australian Academic and Research Network (AARNet) in 1989 greatly improved the speed and reliability of inter-institutional data communications. A nationally funded project, the Australian Distance Education Network (ADENet) Project, put banks of modems into designated institutions

Table 6.1   *Checklist of features to look for in integrated electronic learning environments*

Feature	Notes
Asynchronous conferencing	
☐ Supports threading	Allows students to follow the sequence of a series of messages on a topic
☐ Allows formation of groups by subject/ module	
Synchronous conferencing	
☐ Provides cross-platform whiteboard support	
☐ Supports application sharing	
Mail	
☐ Supports SMTP	Allows exchange of mail with other servers across the Internet
☐ Supports POP	Allows mail to be retrieved by mail clients such as Eudora that use Post Office Protocol
☐ Supports creation of personal mail lists	
Learning management	
☐ Delivers learning materials developed using a range of authoring software	
☐ Tracks progress of students	
☐ Directs students' study route based on their performance on tests	
Testing	
☐ Supports a comprehensive range of item types including algorithmic	
☐ Supports random selection of items	
☐ Allows the timing of tests to be set	
☐ Reports results of a given student on a test	
☐ Reports results of all students on a given test	
Database	
☐ Supports inclusion of interactive multimedia segments programmed in common authoring systems	
☐ Allows open access for import and export of course-related and student-related data	

in major population centres specifically for the use of distance education students (Atkinson and Castro, 1991).

With the growing awareness of the importance of information technology, the Australian government became increasingly interested in encouraging the use of computers. Equity of opportunity also became an important issue at this time. The government was keen to use technology to give better access to education to those who lived in remote and isolated areas. A central service was established to provide access to open learning and distance education students.

Finally, with the advent of the World Wide Web and the deregulation of the telecommunication industry, a market was established for Internet service providers (ISPs). ISPs charged by the hour. However, their rates were generally much lower than those for long-distance calls.

The rise of the ISPs has eliminated an intractable problem. Most institutions had been finding that no sooner had they increased the number of lines, demand increased to meet the new level of supply. Institutions simply could not afford to provide the number of modems needed to service all their students. The ISPs now provide a point of access where it is needed – at the local level.

ISPs are able to respond quickly to increased demand by installing more modems. Since the appearance of ISPs, we have seen a rapid increase in the speed of uptake of new communication standards. No sooner were 56 kbps modems available on the market than ISPs began offering a 56 kbps service.

Already some institutions are closing down their dial-in services and moving across to ISP access for undergraduate programmes. Some institutions see this as a way of shifting more of the cost of provision onto the student. However, other institutions recognize that there are issues of equity here. In fact, the issue of whether the student or the provider should bear the cost of access is a separate question. However, if an institution enters into a contract with an ISP then its enormous buying power can enable it to obtain very attractive rates. Furthermore, by registering students as a group, an institution can greatly reduce the real cost of providing the service, leading to further reductions in the price being charged.

It is inevitable that as the use of the Internet grows, having an Internet access account will be as commonplace as having a telephone account. Indeed, it is not inconceivable that telephone services will eventually be subsumed within a much expanded Internet. However, for the present, we need to accept that subscribing to an ISP is seen by most people as a considerable investment and for many the perceived benefits of Internet access do not justify the cost. Any steps that a provider takes to reduce the cost and simplify the process of gaining Internet access will be likely to lead to an increase in the number of subscribers.

Upgrading local networks

Most educational institutions have accepted that if they are to be able to support delivery of Web and multimedia materials they are going to have to upgrade their communications infrastructure. However, those educational managers who lack a background in data communications are experiencing difficulty in knowing where to start, what priorities to assign to different tasks and what level of funding to allocate.

The key to understanding the nature of the problem is to recognize the magnitude of the increase in the load on networks being brought about by Web traffic. Most existing networks have been dimensioned to cope with network traffic which comprises a mix of e-mail, access to word-processed files and databases, and distributed use of software. Using the existing networks as the conduits for multimedia distribution places a load on them that they were not designed to carry.

Some feeling for the scale of the problem can be gained when it is realized that a full colour image typically generates more than ten times as much data as the equivalent area of text. Yet most Web sites make extensive use of colour images whereas most e-mail messages are only a few lines long.

Local area networks have become like the streets of Bangkok. They are clogged with network traffic, greatly increasing the length of time involved in accessing information held on servers, increasing the level of frustration and decreasing the productivity of network users.

The solution to the problem is not to replace complete networks or even to duplicate them. It is to relieve the 'pressure points'. Just as putting in motorways and roundabouts can get the traffic on other roads moving again, so increasing the capacity of network backbones and upgrading routers and servers can restore networks to an acceptable level of performance. Further improvements can be made by distributing servers so that their location is matched to their use. However, getting the network traffic flowing again does not guarantee that it will remain that way. Arriving at a design that will continue to provide adequate performance for the foreseeable future depends on knowing what future traffic patterns are likely to be.

The principles of network design are relatively simple but the design of networks can be quite complex. Added to that, networks are continually having to be reconfigured so as to accommodate additional equipment. The way in which one approaches the design of a network depends very much on the purpose for which it is being designed. The designers of a network therefore need to have an understanding of the way in which it will be used.

Just as educational managers have difficulty understanding bits and bytes, network managers have difficulty in understanding the distinction between facilitating learning and transmitting information. Network managers are information technologists. They are trained to see the function of networks as transmitting information. How the educational developments are likely to affect the pattern of information flows is not something that they are trained to know. If network support staff are to anticipate them, then they need to be made equal partners in the planning process.

Work stations

Many of the problems that beset teachers in the use of computers result from the fact that the equipment they are required to use is not sufficiently up to date.

It is unfortunately the case that many educational institutions simply do not make adequate provision in their annual budgets for regular replacement and upgrading of desktop computers. Computers are replaced when they fail or when the cost of maintaining them becomes too high. Yet the cost of the staff time that is lost in trying to cope with inadequate equipment may be higher than the total cost of replacement. If this is the case, an institution's resources are not being managed appropriately.

Upgrading too quickly can also be a problem. In the computer industry it is quite common for problems to emerge with a new system in the first few months following its release. Early adopters pay the price of their pioneering role. They also buy their equipment more expensively because computer manufacturers seek to recover the costs of development in the first year.

Managing the information technology infrastructure effectively therefore involves allocating sufficient funds so that it is possible to maintain a regular replacement programme matched to developments in both the market and the needs of the organization.

Summary

Re-engineering the technological infrastructure of an education or training provider for online and interactive multimedia delivery should start with the development of a clear understanding of what's to be achieved. The types of changes that are likely to be needed will lie in three main areas:

- acquisition and implementation of new systems for managing the delivery of courses in an online environment of which the most important will be an integrated electronic learning environment;
- acquisition of software for courseware development; and
- updating the computer and communications infrastructure of the organization to support the greater load on networks and systems.

Broadly speaking, there are three alternative approaches that may be taken to implementing an electronic learning environment:

1. custom design – build a system from the ground up;
2. off-the-shelf – acquire a licence to one of the commercially available systems;
3. building block – combine components from different suppliers.

The approach that will be most appropriate in any particular situation will depend on the goals and circumstances of the provider.

A central component of an integrated electronic learning environment is a learning management system. The type of learning management system that is most appropriate for a particular situation will depend on whether the curriculum is structured and based on subject matter elements, or based on competencies. Most learning management systems currently available are based on subject matter.

The upgrading of information technology infrastructure to support online and multimedia delivery will involve a major initial investment in hardware and software. These facilities will also require continual upgrading. The re-designing of information technology infrastructure will also need to become an ongoing process.

Chapter 7

Re-skilling and supporting staff

We commence this chapter by suggesting how to create a work environment suitable for staff working with the knowledge media. We go on to identify the knowledge and skills that staff will require. We suggest ways of assessing and recording the current computer proficiency of staff and determining their development needs. We then examine the range of alternative forms that staff development may take and make suggestions for choosing between them in setting up a comprehensive staff development programme.

Creating an appropriate work environment

In any work environment there are many factors that contribute to staff commitment and to staff acting competently, creatively and responsibly. These include motivation, indications of being valued, interpersonal relationships, having shared goals and clear and open communications. Here we take up a point particularly pertinent to introducing knowledge media: how you create the conditions for staff to work effectively with these media.

There are some general considerations that can be explored in seeking to provide appropriate and satisfactory working conditions for staff engaged in the design, development and delivery of knowledge media. These include:

- location of offices and work areas;
- electronic communication networks;
- equipment and software access requirements;
- health, safety and comfort requirements;
- recognition and reward systems.

The physical proximity of staff involved in the design, development and delivery of knowledge media may not appear to be an issue when the medium of delivery is electronic. There remain, however, advantages in co-locating staff involved in the design and development of knowledge media. The development of understanding, the raising and solving of incidental issues and the generation of creative approaches can be best served by arrangements that allow staff to interact in an unplanned, incidental and informal form. Not all interested parties can be co-located and those involved may change on a project-by-project basis. One solution is to provide a product design and development area in which space can be shared by those involved in a particular project at the times they are engaged on it.

One issue that often arises is the advantages and disadvantages of open-planned office arrangements against individual offices. Separate offices can provide confidentiality in conversations, which could sometimes be appropriate in discussions between designers and teaching staff. It is important to have an office area that has sound insulation from multimedia audio output, which can be very distracting, particularly when the same sound effect is being repeatedly tested in the development phases. Separate offices, however, can lessen the advantages of co-location. A compromise is to provide separate withdrawal areas for private conversations, sound insulated areas for multimedia development and open-plan offices for other activities. Adaptation to the environment may require a cultural shift for those involved.

Providing adequate and appropriate network access is vital for design and development which includes access to Intranets and the Internet. Security checks may be needed to protect confidential materials against unauthorized access.

Staff obviously require access to work stations that have sufficient speed and memory to perform the functions required of them, and to suitable and up-to-date software. One of the issues is: does everyone involved need to be issued personally with each item of equipment and every item of software? The test is access. Access needs to be available within a time frame in which the costs of any delays (eg, the cost of unproductive staff time, or the costs incurred or income opportunities lost through delayed delivery times) do not exceed the costs of providing the equipment and software. You may also wish to use the provision of a better standard of equipment as part of a reward or motivation system.

Occupational health and safety requirements, including ventilation in areas in which electronic equipment, particularly photocopying and printing, is operating, need to be taken into account. Ergonomic furniture needs to be provided. Comfort considerations might go beyond minimal requirements.

Where use of knowledge media is seen as an add-on activity, it may not be regarded in a fashion that encourages participation and innovation. In particular the staff work load involved in the design and development of the media needs to be recognized. Conducting courses employing digital media also needs to be recognized in the same way as classroom teaching is.

Knowledge media may be developed to supplement classroom activities. The development of the digital resources may have taken considerable staff time and initiative but, while the quality of the learning experiences and options may have been enhanced, the number of students taught may remain the same. It can be difficult to arrange appropriate operational recognition in these circumstances. An alternative is to offer one-off rewards such as project funding or including teaching innovation as a criteria for promotion. This, incidentally, raises questions about the desirability of developing knowledge media as a supplement to classroom activities. You cannot afford to continue committing resources to developments that make no difference to the costs of delivery or to income – though some institutions do. Through giving some thought to design, development and delivery, media innovations can replace some of the commitment of resources to the classroom.

What new skills will staff need?

The employment of digital technologies for the provision of educational and training programmes requires sets of expertise, some of which are very new. Indeed, the range of expertise that education and training providers need in order to support these new media is continually changing as technologies develop and software is updated. This expertise can be acquired by:

- recruitment;
- staff development; or
- buying-in or contracting-out.

The recency of many learning technologies means that established staff may lack capabilities important to exploiting the potential of the technologies. Recruitment may be an option, provided what is recruited is not just current know-how but a capacity to adapt to technological change. You can't recruit experience in tomorrow's technology.

Because the expertise required is of recent origin it is often in short supply. Development programmes for suitable staff provide a solution where expertise is difficult to recruit. Staff development in a changing environment is necessary but can have a downside. The capabilities that staff acquire through staff development will make them more marketable. There is, therefore, a risk that they will leave. Technical staff, in particular, are often subject to high turnover. On the other hand, there is an inertia factor which tends to reduce the frequency of staff movements. Nevertheless, you need to look to ensuring work satisfaction for expert staff and appropriate levels of remuneration or provision of other rewards.

If the expertise is required only occasionally it may be most economical to buy-in or to contract-out the particular tasks. This practice can also make staff turnover and industrial relations somebody else's problem. However, it is important to recognize the intellectual property implications of outsourcing; these were discussed in Chapter 5.

By one means or another new staff capabilities are required. Which staff need which abilities? Knowledge media create new staff relationships in education and training enterprises. The degree to which it is best for staff to specialize is taken up in Chapter 8. What we can say here is that all staff – administrative, technical,

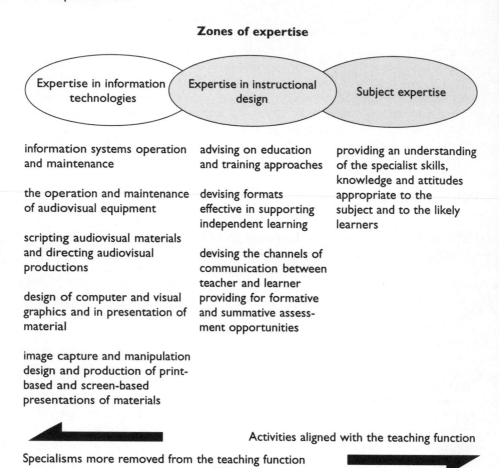

Figure 7.1 *Organising for digital delivery*

audio–visual, library, instructional design and teaching – contribute to the design, development and operation of knowledge media and that roles cannot be quarantined. Technicians need a feel for pedagogical principles; teachers need an appreciation of technical possibilities and limitations; student administrators need some appreciation of the tuition processes and instructional design involved. Teachers and multimedia designers need to work with librarians to optimize access to resources. Different roles have different emphases but the boundaries overlap and each specialist requires the contribution of the others, as indicated in Figure 7.1.

Assessing the computer proficiency of teaching staff

There is, then, no simple answer to the question of what skills and knowledge staff need in order to work effectively with new learning technologies. Nor is

Table 7.1   *Computer skills audit checklist*

Key to columns:
1. I have no skills or limited skills in this area
2. I have developed skills in this area
3. Skills confirmed by audit

NAME _____

	Column		
	1	2	3
Environment PC or Macintosh			
Operating in Windows environment or on Macintosh desktop	❏	❏	❏
Organizing files and data	❏	❏	❏
Word processing & desktop publishing			
eg MS Word, Pagemaker			
Handling files, eg find file, open, save, page setup, print	❏	❏	❏
Editing, eg copy, paste, find & replace	❏	❏	❏
Viewing files, eg using toolbars and headers	❏	❏	❏
Inserting, eg pictures, dates, annotations, page nos	❏	❏	❏
Formatting, eg fonts, borders, bullet points & nos	❏	❏	❏
Using tools, eg spell check, auto-correct, macros	❏	❏	❏
Using columns, eg 2 columns, frames, callouts	❏	❏	❏
Using tables, eg creating tables, auto format, sort data	❏	❏	❏
Spreadsheets eg MS Excel			
Handling files, eg find file, open, save, page setup, print	❏	❏	❏
Editing, eg copy, paste, find & replace	❏	❏	❏
Entering data in worksheets and workbooks	❏	❏	❏
Writing formulas, eg add/multiply/etc items, ranges, formulas, statistical functions, scenarios	❏	❏	❏
Formatting, eg data as $s, borders, colour, autoformats	❏	❏	❏
Charting data, eg pie charts, graphs	❏	❏	❏
Data management, eg sort, worksheet management, reports	❏	❏	❏
Linking data to other programs	❏	❏	❏
Automating repetitive tasks using toolbars and macros	❏	❏	❏
Presentation software eg MS PowerPoint			
Handling files, eg find file, open, save, page setup, print	❏	❏	❏
Editing, eg copy, paste, find & replace	❏	❏	❏
Viewing, eg slides, notes, outlines, toolbars	❏	❏	❏
Inserting, eg slides, arts, graphs, movies, page nos	❏	❏	❏
Formatting, eg fonts, bullet points, templates, colour schemes	❏	❏	❏
Using tools, eg spell check, slide shows	❏	❏	❏
Drawing, eg shapes, colouring, grouping, sizing, positioning	❏	❏	❏
Slide show, eg animate, transition, build, buttons	❏	❏	❏
Databases eg Filemaker, Access			
Handling files, eg find file, open, save, page setup, print	❏	❏	❏
Designing databases, eg fields	❏	❏	❏
Entering and modifying data in databases	❏	❏	❏
Formatting, eg data as $s, form layout	❏	❏	❏
Data management, eg sort, reports, calculated fields	❏	❏	❏
Linking data to other programs	❏	❏	❏

Table 7.1   *(continued)*

Ideas software eg Inspiration			
Handling files, eg find file, open, save, page setup, print	❑	❑	❑
Editing, eg copy, paste, change symbols & links	❑	❑	❑
Viewing files, eg schema, outline, text, headers	❑	❑	❑
Concept mapping, eg ideas, symbols, links	❑	❑	❑
Formatting, eg fonts, colours	❑	❑	❑
Using tools, eg spellcheck, find & replace	❑	❑	❑
E-mail eg Eudora, Pegasus			
Sending & receiving mail	❑	❑	❑
Using lists, eg subscribe, unsubscribe, address lists	❑	❑	❑
Attachments, eg sending & receiving attachments	❑	❑	❑
Web browsers eg Netscape Navigator, MS Explorer			
Handling files, eg open browser, save, page setup, print	❑	❑	❑
Editing, eg copy, paste, find & replace	❑	❑	❑
Searching using search engines	❑	❑	❑
Searching online, eg library catalogue, telephone directories	❑	❑	❑
Bookmarking	❑	❑	❑
Options, eg fonts, colour, mail preferences, toolbars	❑	❑	❑
Navigating, eg hypertext, forward, back	❑	❑	❑
Web authoring software eg FrontPage, Pagemill			
Handling files, eg open, publish, import	❑	❑	❑
Edit, eg copy, paste, to do tasks	❑	❑	❑
Viewing, eg toolbars, status bars, hyperlinks	❑	❑	❑
Using tools, eg spelling, hyperlinks, web settings	❑	❑	❑

there a simple answer to which staff need which skills and knowledge. However, in an organization committed to the application of the knowledge media, there are minimal technological competencies that teaching staff should be capable of displaying. Table 7.1 gives a checklist of the basic computer skills and aptitudes that staff involved in courseware development are likely to require.

The skills, knowledge and attitudes required of staff go well beyond the minimums indicated in Table 7.1. Figure 7.1 gives an indication of other areas in which staff development may be required. The areas which are appropriate to your situation need to be defined and the competencies in each area specified. A profile of current competencies can be derived by audit, perhaps using a format similar to that used in Table 7.1. This can then be used to determine your specific staff development requirements.

Forms of staff development

Staff development can take many forms. Those that are commonly used include:

- training;
- seminars and workshops;
- mentoring;

- staff-initiated innovation projects;
- quality improvement processes.

Some of these staff development activities may be conducted in-house while others may be conducted by outside providers.

Training sessions

The conduct of a training programme may be an appropriate approach to staff development in a situation where an enabling skill, such as the ability to operate the basic commands of a particular software package, is required and where immediate benefit can be obtained from application of the skill. However, a 'how to' training approach is not likely to be appropriate, at least by itself, if judgement needs to be exercised in the application of the skill, or if conditions for application are uncertain or are subject to change.

Seminars and workshops

Seminars and workshops provide scope for participants to contribute solutions and exchange ideas. Presentations at a seminar may have some influence but, to produce change, seminars need to involve the opportunity to practise skills, to reflect upon the application of information to the work context, and to relate theory and practice over time. To have wide impact across the organization, a programme of seminars and workshops needs to be closely linked to the organization's strategic plans and work programme. Seminars and workshops pertinent to and attended by all staff of a department are more likely to generate changes than those attended by a few.

Mentoring

Mentoring can be an effective means of staff development both for newly recruited staff and for existing staff. In either case commitment is required of both mentor and mentee. The commitment of the mentee may arise from a need to know. The selection of people with an interest in the process is important in obtaining mentors with commitment. This is most likely to occur with a structured and monitored process involving a formal mentoring agreement, with agreed aims and objectives, procedures such as observation arrangements and meeting times, an agreed form of record keeping such as a journal, agreed regular forms of communication, and an agreed system of monitoring and evaluation of the relationship and its processes.

Staff initiatives

Support or stimulation of staff initiatives may also be a means to staff development. Provision of financial or other support for innovative projects, as well as resulting in a product, can also lead to the development of expertise.

The history of generating change in educational organizations in the direction of greater use of the knowledge media is not encouraging. There have been some outstanding successes, but for many, more thought goes into the process of obtaining funding support than into the educational initiative. Those who are successful in obtaining funding invariably find the task more demanding in time and energy than anticipated. Many projects never reach completion, systematic evaluation is lacking and communication of the results of the projects beyond the project teams is limited. When the enthusiasts who have been responsible for initiating a project move on, the project is abandoned. This is not to say that valuable learning and development may not have occurred during the processes, just that more is usually expected of such projects by both sponsors and innovators than is delivered. To maximize benefits it is important to:

- make a realistic estimate of the resources required for design, development and delivery;
- evaluate systematically;
- ensure the innovation is adopted by selecting or developing projects integral to courses or departments' programmes and that fit with the strategic plan.

Quality improvement processes

Staff development may also occur by the adoption of quality improvement processes that require reflection, evaluation, plans for improvement, actions and further evaluation. Student evaluation of courses, for instance, may suggest areas of programmes that could do with improving. A systematic approach to student evaluation of courses will provide for analysis of responses and reporting of findings, planned actions and outcomes. It will allow staff to reflect on findings and to plan for staff development.

Designing a staff development programme

The focus of staff development programmes

A focus on staff development as a key to the adaptation of education and training organizations to the digital age, is an acknowledgement that staff, along with customers, clients, suppliers and other people who interact with an organization, constitute the organization. They not only constitute the organization in a similar way to its buildings and other resources but, through their perceptions of the organization, and hence the way in which they relate to it, they help to constitute what the organization is and how it operates.

Organizational change and adaptation depend on the development of staff. The development of staff changes the perceptions and understandings they have of the organization and consequently the nature of the organization. As an organization changes its staff it changes itself. The changes that take place may be unintended as well as intended.

Staff development programmes, therefore, need to have an institutional orientation to them. They are not only about technical developments and possibilities or even educational creativity. Staff need to have a clear understanding of institutional missions and goals in relation to the knowledge media. Staff development should be strategically related to course development and delivery priorities.

Staff development programmes also need to provide staff with a clear understanding of the principles underpinning the use of digital delivery technologies and an appreciation of the potential of those technologies.

Tailoring a person's development programme to their role

In devising a staff development programme to enhance digital delivery, the first point that needs to be established is which staff are to be developed, what their roles are and what their development requirements are. While there may be benefits in all staff involved in the design, development and application of the knowledge media having an appreciation of the processes as a whole, it is important to be clear about the role expected and to focus development efforts upon this. In particular there is little point in training all teaching staff to design and develop multimedia if specialists are employed to carry out this function. What is required of teachers, apart from keeping up to date in their subject area, is understanding of learning and teaching and the ability to translate the understanding into effective teaching and learning transactions. Thereafter they might benefit from some attention to the areas of expertise most proximate to the teaching function as indicated in Figure 7.1.

For instructional designers and for technical staff, the focus of their staff development will be the areas of their specialism. However, roles are not static. They need to be adapted to accommodate developments in technology. The convergence of audio-visual and computing technologies is leading to marked shifts in what have previously been established and defined role boundaries. For example, a photographer's role once had almost nothing to do with computing. Photographic chemistry is now rapidly being replaced by digital technology and computers are being used to capture, store, manipulate and use digital images. Staff who prepare print-based material must now be able to work with digital templates, if not design them. These changes in work and working environment require staff development responses.

It could be argued that as approaches to education and training move toward greater flexibility in time, place and pace for learners there is also a convergence between education provision and the media and multimedia industry. Traditional educational enterprises are adopting new modes of delivery while media and software corporations market education and training products. This does not necessarily mean that the roles of educators and trainers will be conflated with those of media designers and developers. If the enterprises are large enough they will maintain specialist roles.

Selecting the right form of staff development

A staff development programme will utilize multiple forms of staff development. The form of staff development you will find most effective for meeting a particular need will depend on the skills that are required and the staff member or staff members who require them. Approaches likely to be most successful are those that involve all personnel in a work group, generating a commitment to change and creating a common understanding of the directions of change and the means to attain it. Working with teaching teams or with departments as a whole is likely to be more successful than drawing individuals from across an organization.

For new staff, the most appropriate form of staff development may be mentoring.

Should participation in staff development be voluntary or compulsory?

Compulsory or obligatory participation in staff development is not likely to produce an enthusiastic response. Nor is it likely to lead to a worthwhile development of the staff member's knowledge and skills. On the other hand, leaving participation to individual whim is not likely to serve institutional needs either. Participation in staff development programmes should be strategic – tied to individual performance planning, relating it to position descriptions and integrating it into promotion and reward systems.

Summary

In preparing staff to deliver courses via the knowledge media, you should first consider what changes are required to their work environment. Aspects that should be reviewed include:

- location of offices and work areas;
- communications facilities;
- equipment and software;
- health, safety and comfort;
- recognition and reward systems.

In proceeding to devise a staff development programme you should begin by making an assessment of the existing skills of staff against the range of new skills that you know will be needed. From this assessment you should then identify which skills are 'missing'. The staff development programme can then be constructed using a combination of different strategies:

- training sessions;
- seminars and workshops;
- mentoring;
- staff-initiated innovation projects;
- quality improvement processes.

Chapter 8

Reorienting the teaching programme

In this chapter we:

- distinguish between some alternative approaches to teaching that may be employed in delivering programmes via the knowledge media;
- identify the implications of each approach;
- examine the relative merits of designing and developing courseware compared with acquiring courseware produced elsewhere;
- provide a set of criteria and a checklist for selecting courseware;
- examine the advantages of entering into collaborative ventures in the design, development and adaptation of courseware.

Approaches to teaching with the knowledge media

There is a variety of ways in which courses can be delivered digitally. Some involve the use of self-contained learning packages and some involve ongoing teacher–learner or learner–learner communication. The self-contained approach tends to maximize time, pace and place flexibility for both teachers and learners but is relatively static in content and in the learning approach once it is adopted. This option therefore implies a carefully researched and designed product. Computer mediated communication between teachers and learners and between learners and learners allows somewhat less time, pace and place flexibility, particularly if the communication is synchronous. It is, however, more dynamic and flexible in its ability to respond to individual and group learning needs as learning progresses. It does not require that the needs of multiple learners be anticipated. It requires instead an ongoing capacity to generate learning and to react to learning

Table 8.1 *A simple typology of approaches to digital delivery*

	Time, pace and place flexibility	Adaptability to learning needs	Investment of time
Self-contained learning packages	High	Low	Higher design and development costs
Computer mediated communication	Lower, particularly where synchronous	High	Higher operating costs

developments. The characteristics of the different approaches are summarized in Table 8.1.

Of course a combination of these approaches may be adopted to provide for learner needs and organizational requirements. Either of the approaches may be combined with elements of face-to-face tuition to meet learner needs and preferences. Such combinations might be facilitated by the use of computer-managed learning systems. We move on to look at the basic approaches first and then to consider combinations, including computer-managed learning.

Self-contained learning packages

In this approach, the courseware more or less stands alone. Typically this might take the form of a complete module on CD ROM or a module presented on a self-contained Web site.

Adoption of this approach assumes that the learning needs and prior learning of the target group of learners can be anticipated and accommodated. It is, however, difficult to produce courseware which matches the full spectrum of learner characteristics. Courseware that suits some learners often may not suit others. If a learning package is going to be effective as a self-instructional medium, then considerable attention needs to be paid to its design. Learner requirements and learner characteristics need to be researched. It is important to trial and evaluate the product during the design and development stages to make adjustments for the way learners behave with the digital materials.

Once learning needs have been established, the design of self-contained learning packages should ensure that:

- the intended learning outcomes are explicit;
- the materials are logically and transparently structured;
- alternative starting points, pathways and end-points are offered;
- each segment of the program incorporates an element of self-assessment;
- the materials are attractive and easy to navigate.

The initial costs of research, design, development and evaluation are high – especially for courseware involving multimedia. Self-contained learning packages are therefore most suited to use with large numbers of students.

The variable costs associated with delivery, on the other hand, can be substantially reduced in the case of fully self-contained learning packages. Self-contained materials imply no tutorial support and the costs of reproduction and distribution of materials are minor components of the overall cost. The high up-front costs of design and development may be recouped from the resulting savings. The use of self-contained learning packages, however, cannot completely eliminate variable costs of delivery. There may still be significant costs associated with student enrolment, administrative support and student assessment.

Self-contained learning packages are most suited to situations where:

- the potential market for a new course is large;
- flexibility with regard to time, place and pace is of prime importance;
- the characteristics of the learners in the target group are known or can be readily ascertained;
- materials can be trialed during the design and development phases;
- learners in the target group have other learning materials and facilities on which they can draw.

Computer-mediated communication

An alternative approach to using packaged self-instructional materials is to use computers to facilitate online discussion, exchange and provision of information. Such communication was originally text-based but it can now include sound, graphics and video. The interaction may be:

- one-to-one – providing individually pertinent communication;
- one-to-many – allowing economy of communication to the instigator of the communication;
- many-to-many – allowing multiple participants to contribute to or to audit the communication.

This online communication may utilize a variety of means:

- e-mail;
- listservs;
- electronic bulletin boards;
- newsgroups;
- Web-based conferencing systems, including threaded discussions and Internet relayed chat;
- dedicated educational conferencing systems;
- desktop conferencing with text, graphics, databases, spreadsheets, voice, whiteboard and/or video;

- MUDs (Multi-user Dimensions, Dungeons, or Dialogues) which allow participants to 'chat' or take actions in pursuit of a task.

The interaction may use asynchronous forms of communication, that is forms in which the responses to messages are delayed (eg, e-mail and threaded discussions) or synchronous forms, that is forms in which responses to messages are made immediately (eg, 'chat' sessions or desktop video conferencing).

Asynchronous communication provides time and pace flexibility, allowing participants to give considered responses at a time that suits them. On the other hand, asynchronous communication forms can be a protracted means of interaction between teachers and learners, between fellow learners, and between learners and resource personnel. They are best employed where participants have differing time availability, where participation in the communication is optional in the learning situation, or where response requires consideration or investigation. Asynchronous electronic communication may also be set up to provide anonymity to participants. This can be of value, for instance in encouraging reluctant learners to participate.

Synchronous conferencing offers a greater sense of participation but demands more spontaneity. Synchronous and asynchronous conferencing refer to two ends of a spectrum rather than being mutually exclusive. E-mail, for example, can be used semi-synchronously.

The major advantages of online communication are that:

- it allows teachers to respond flexibly to the changing needs, abilities and understanding of individual learners;
- teachers and other learners may be used as resources;
- learners can explore each others' meaning and understanding.

The use of computer-mediated communication may lead to higher costs if it increases the extent of direct teacher–learner interaction. Digital communication may, however, be organized in ways that contain costs. It may be used to increase learner–learner interaction without much teacher input. Computer-mediated communication may be set up to allow a teacher to monitor interactions between learners and to intervene only occasionally, for example to counter misconceptions, to motivate and stimulate learning, or to change direction or open new paths for consideration.

Integrated electronic learning environments, such as Learning Space, TopClass, FirstClass and WebCT, which were described in Chapter 6, generally provide their own support for computer-mediated communication. General purpose business communications software or 'groupware', such as Lotus Notes or Groupwise, provide many of the same functions and can also be utilized. Using the same communication software for both teaching and administrative purposes has many advantages. It makes fewer demands on institutional infrastructure, and it requires less skill development on the part of both staff and students. On the other hand it has limitations. Induction to communications software and the operation of software involves the use of metaphors such as mailboxes, documents and bulletin boards. The metaphors employed for administrative purposes, such as filing cabinets, often differ from those used for educational purposes, such as online libraries. Sometimes a metaphor refers to an aggregation of functions as is the case for the virtual classroom.

Metaphors matter in conceptualizing the uses to which the software may be put and the protocols and conventions that govern their use. While the same software base may be used for administrative and educational purposes, there may be value in using alternative descriptors or icons for at least some functions.

Combining approaches

The two approaches to course delivery that have been described above – self-contained packages and computer-mediated exchanges – are basic forms. Generally, the construction of a course will involve a combination of these approaches. The use of computer-mediated exchanges alone is seldom sufficient as a means of facilitating learning. Discussion needs to be combined with other learning activities and the use of learning resources. On the other hand, difficulty in anticipating learner needs in the development of self-contained packages can be compensated for by providing opportunities for person-to-person interaction. The weight given to each component will determine the character of the course.

In a course that is primarily delivered via computer-mediated communication or in a course primarily delivered face-to-face, packaged self-instructional materials may be used to:

● illustrate a concept;
● supplement learning experiences appropriate to the skills, knowledge, attitudes and propensities that students are expected to develop;
● provide simulations of learning experiences too expensive, inconvenient or hazardous to provide otherwise;
● provide some motivating variation in teaching approach.

In a course that is largely based on self-contained learning materials, computer-mediated communication might be used to:

● introduce learning materials to the particular learners and explain their purposes and procedures;
● monitor students' development of concepts and skills and to adjust the presentation of a course accordingly;
● respond to learner concerns arising from the materials;
● support learning through peer interaction;
● update or supplement materials.

In choosing to combine approaches economic, pragmatic, competitive and even political aspects need to be taken into account. The most important factor to be considered is how the learners who will be taking the course are best likely to achieve the outcome intended. There are differing views but one thing is agreed – the simple presentation of information is not likely to be the optimal approach. Approaches likely to be favoured are those that:

- make objectives explicit;
- involve learners in a process they see as relevant to their learning needs;
- involve the learners in making decisions and undertaking actions;
- can be monitored by a learning facilitator;
- allow intervention and interaction between participants.

Using a computer-based learning management system

Learning management systems, such as The Learning Manager, direct learners to learning resources, administer computer-scored tests, track students' progress and determine the pace at which the learner progresses and the path he or she follows. As explained in Chapter 6, some integrated electronic learning environments provide facilities for learning management. These systems are potentially able to perform the full range of course delivery functions.

Computer-based learning management systems (CML) were developed in the mid-1970s. The original CML systems were not able to deliver courseware; they merely directed the learner to resources that were available in other media, such as print or video. This limitation existed because of the restricted capacity of computer storage media of the time. Now that storage capacity is cheap, most learning resources can be delivered in digital form (although copyright restrictions may preclude the electronic delivery of published material). Also, because many aspects of the administration of a course can be streamlined or automated, the efficiency with which a course is delivered can be considerably increased.

Using a learning management system increases the degree of flexibility that can be built into courses. Rather than requiring all learners to follow the same path through a programme, using a modular structure, learning management systems tailor the pathway that the learner takes according to individual needs. Modules may direct learners to alternative resources such as print, video, course-ware and even appropriately scheduled face-to-face activities such as supervised practice.

Because courses delivered by means of a CML are constructed in a modular fashion, individual components of a programme can be added, modified or deleted without affecting the remainder of the programme. Courses are therefore more easily kept up-to-date than those based on self-contained courseware.

To manage the pace at which learners progress and the pathway they follow, learning management systems rely on the results of regular tests. Courses that are based on the use of learning management systems may therefore be seen as 'assessment driven' – but so is much formal education and training. This is not necessarily a problem if the assessment is appropriate to the learning needs and the learning outcomes that are sought.

If computer-scored tests are used, care needs to be taken with the design of test items. There is a risk that teachers and trainers who are not skilled in writing test items will limit the items they write to the easier-to-construct forms. These tend to test lower-order learning outcomes such as recall of information. However, with careful design, computer-scored tests are capable of measuring higher-order learning outcomes such as explanation, comparison, analysis, synthesis and hypothesising. Learning management systems can also accept the results of assessment that have not been administered by computer.

A learning management system is best suited to situations in which:

- time, place and pace flexibility are considered of prime importance;
- a variety of learning resources is employed;
- staff development in the appropriate use of the system and the design of test items and curricula can be provided.

Economies of scale can be obtained by extending use of the learning management system across several courses.

Approaches and the role of the provider

In discussing the rationales for shifting to the knowledge media we pointed out that stand-alone materials maximize time, place and pace flexibility for learners. If, however, an organization produces nothing but fully stand-alone digital materials, with no assessment of students' work or other form of teacher–learner interaction, it acts as an electronic publishing house rather than as an educational institution. At the other extreme, to rely solely on direct teacher–learner interaction is to fail to utilize the potential and flexibility offered by digital media. It is a matter of striking an effective and efficient balance.

If we wish to retain our roles as educational or training providers, we need at the least to retain the function of student accreditation; that is, we need to assess students' work and certify progress. Of course we could decide to have it both ways by offering accreditation as an option and marketing materials on a fully stand-alone basis to individuals or to other education and training providers.

Should courseware be developed or acquired?

If you plan to adopt an approach involving courseware, you need to decide whether to engage in the design and development of courseware within your institution or to adopt or adapt existing courseware. The decision rests on a number of factors; key among them are:

- Is the market large or small?
- Is the subject matter specialized?

- What is the shelf-life of the courseware?
- What are the costs of any necessary copyright clearances?

Size of the market

If the size of the market or extent of the user group you are intending to tap is small, then you will not be able to obtain the maximum economies of scale that are potentially available (see Chapter 4). The costs of courseware development will be high in relation to the costs of delivery. You will find it much more economical in this case to use materials produced elsewhere than to develop your own, if suitable materials are available.

Specialization

If the field of study you are targeting is popular, then there is likely to be a wealth of courseware already available for purchase or licensing. This would be the case, for example, in a field such as business statistics or basic topics in physics. In this case you are likely to find that you can obtain access to suitable courseware at a cost that is considerably lower than developing courseware yourself. On the other hand, if the field of study is quite specialized, then there may be no alternative but to develop your own materials. However, even in a specialized field of study, it may be more economical to supplement existing material than to start from scratch. For example, a module in viticulture for local climate and soil conditions might not be readily obtainable on the market but a digital module on viticulture may be available and an electronic or print-based supplement to draw out the consequences for local conditions might be prepared.

Shelf-life

The frequency with which design and development will need to be undertaken affects the choice between developing materials, collaborating in development of materials, or purchasing or otherwise acquiring available products.

The concept of shelf-life is most pertinent to largely stand-alone courseware. Traditionally, print-based distance education course materials, which are designed to be largely stand-alone, have been expected to have a shelf-life of five years. There is usually some allowance for updating and minor modification in this period. In some fields of study, such as taxation law, substantial revisions are required each year. The rate of change in knowledge, the availability of constantly changing information, the rate of change in technologies, a climate of frequent upgrading of software, and the moves of competitors in an increasingly globalized education and training environment, suggest that shelf-life should be reduced, perhaps to three years.

The shelf-life can be maximized where the courseware, rather than containing current information, focuses on:

- appropriate approaches to learning in the area;
- types of learning activities that might be undertaken;
- types of resources that might be tapped;
- simulations and exercises.

The courseware might direct learners to appropriate use of library catalogues, to journal indexes and to topics for Web searches.

While limited shelf-life militates against making a substantial investment in design and development of home-grown materials, it also suggests that substantial investment in commercially available courseware needs to be recouped in a three-year time span, unless the material contains timeless content.

Copyright clearance

A major cost in courseware development can arise from incorporation of materials requiring copyright clearance. Providers engaging in significant amounts of courseware development may need to employ specialist staff to recognize copyright requirements and to identify and negotiate the necessary clearances.

Criteria for selection of courseware

In selecting courseware produced by another provider or by a commercial publisher, a number of considerations need to be taken into account. The environment in which the materials will be used needs to be considered along with whether the materials are to be used as stand-alone or will be teacher-supported. The materials should be appropriate in terms of whom they are designed for and what prior skills and knowledge they presume. The content needs to be appropriate to the learners and organized to facilitate their learning effectively. Multimedia should be used to advantage without distracting from learning. There are advantages in learning packages that monitor usage, allow appropriate assessment of student progress and interface with other approaches to learning. There are delivery matters to consider in terms of hardware requirements, costs and vendor support.

These considerations can be organized into a checklist, such as the one shown in Table 8.2.

Considerations in design and development

Courseware design and development can be very expensive. It is frequently argued that educational consumers of the future will expect sophisticated digital courseware. The commercial computer games industry indicates the potential to develop courseware that requires elaborate research, extensive programming and

Table 8.2 A *checklist for selecting pre-packaged multimedia courseware*

A. Pertinence

☐ Are the materials designed for the intended users?
☐ Are the materials designed for the appropriate instructional context?
(For example: are they designed to be used as self-paced individually used materials or in conjunction with an instructor or together with fellow learners; are they designed to be used in the home, at a workstation, in a laboratory, in a training centre, in a classroom, or in a library or resource centre?)

B. Purpose

☐ Are the learning objectives clear and are the expectations of what the user is to do made clear?
☐ Is the program design systematically related to the learning objectives?

C. Prerequisites

☐ Are the prerequisite knowledge, skills and attitudes made clear and are they appropriate to the intended users?

D. Teaching and learning materials

☐ Are the knowledge, skills and attitudes facilitated appropriate to the intended learners?
☐ Can the key knowledge, skills and attitudes be readily identified?
☐ Does the program provide for increasing levels of complexity
– for example from novice to expert?
☐ Do the materials provide for higher-order learning skills such as problem solving, analysis, synthesis and creativity as against simple recall?
☐ Will the materials be motivating, interesting and challenging for the intended learners?
☐ Do the materials conform to accepted and current understandings in the content area?
☐ Are the materials free from error in expression and in use of terminology?
☐ Are the materials reasonably free from ethnic, gender and political bias?

E. Teaching and learning approach

☐ Is the underlying learning theory apparent and appropriate?
☐ Is there a clear relationship between the learning objectives, the learning activities and the assessment tasks?
☐ Are the intended learning outcomes assessed?
☐ Does progress through the program depend on active/creative actions rather than reaction to set propositions or passive clicking forward?
☐ Are alternative strategies used to meet different learner needs?

Table 8.2   *(continued)*

□ Can activities in the program be extended to face-to-face situations or through other learning materials?

□ Is the learner able to interact with other learners and a teacher or tutor?

F.   Media and navigation

□ Are media such as text, hypertext, graphics, animations, sound, photographs, video used to enhance learning? Is their presence likely to enhance or inhibit learning?

□ Is the quality of media used satisfactory? Is its design appealing? Is text easy to read?

□ Are navigation tools clear, intuitive and consistent? Is the organizing logic of the material apparent to the user and the location of the user in the material apparent? Are tips on how to best use the courseware provided?

□ Is material indexed? Is a glossary of technical terms and abbreviations provided? Is there a search facility? Is there a help facility?

□ Has the material been trialed in relevant circumstances and user behaviours reasonably predicted and allowed for?

□ Can the progress of learners be monitored and tracked and can records be saved and printed?

□ Can the learner make, save and print notes?

G.   Performance

□ Is the speed of the program satisfactory in the hardware and software situation in which it is to be used?

□ Is the program crash-free?

□ Is required hardware and software available?

□ Is installation manageable?

□ Can hardware or software settings be easily restored after use of the program?

H.   Support

□ Are instructor guides available along with supporting teaching aids?

□ Are student guides, activity sheets and the like available?

□ Does the vendor provide training in the use of the materials?

□ Does the vendor provide readily accessible support services?

□ Is the vendor likely to continue in the field?

□ Does the vendor provide upgrades?

I.   Cost-effectiveness

□ Is the use of the courseware likely to be cost-effective against alternative approaches when hardware and software requirements are taken into account along with costs to the user? (See also Chapter 4.)

---

sophisticated graphics and audio. Design and development budgets for such software may run to millions of dollars. There is evidence, however, that students will readily accept courseware developed in-house which lacks aesthetic polish. What they will not accept is courseware that is tedious or difficult to operate.

How can the design of courses contribute to learning effectiveness?

In this book we argue that learning is individual. It is a process that builds on or modifies understanding, capacities, abilities, attitudes and propensities in the individual. This is not to say that people learn best when they learn on their own. On the contrary, learning is often best effected in interaction, whether that interaction be with teachers, mentors or peers, is synchronous or asynchronous, is face-to-face or distant. It is, however, to suggest that where the process involves courseware, the design and development of the courseware should anticipate variety in the circumstances, interests, needs and aptitudes of individual learners.

This implies a number of principles that should be applied in the design and development of courseware. It should:

- either be designed and developed to anticipate the preconditions of the learners, such as their existing range of skills and forms of understanding (including the various ways in which they currently conceptualize a topic), or it should allow the teacher to access the preconditions of the learners and to respond appropriately;
- have time, pace and place flexibility to allow for the various circumstances of the learners such as work and home commitments;
- be designed and developed with the level of the learners' access to learning supports, including educational technology, in mind;
- allow for learning style preferences among users – for instance that some may at times prefer a text-based form while other users, or the same users at other times, may prefer visuals and graphics or kinaesthetic activities;
- provide for formative assessment, possibly through self-assessment tasks and, where courses are taken for credit, for summative assessment. The latter may require invigilated examinations. Experience in distance education indicates that it is usually possible to arrange for invigilated examinations to be taken at a distance. If this is to be done online, close supervision may be needed to ensure no access to unauthorized sources of information;
- allow alternative entry points, levels and depths of tuition, topics and paths, forms of assessment and points of exit;
- allow for partial completion of a session, preferably with a record of progress for each user.

How can the design of courses contribute to learning efficiency?

The general question of costs in the use of new knowledge media was taken up in Chapter 4. One of the conclusions from that chapter was that economies of scale, given the significance of the cost of labour in total cost, depend upon limiting teacher–learner interaction or at least limiting the teaching labour component of teacher and learner interactions.

Limiting teacher–learner interactions is problematic given the desirability from a learning effectiveness point of view of the teacher having an awareness of the circumstances, interests, needs and aptitudes of individual learners, not only initially but on an ongoing basis.

Whether we are focusing on understandings, skills, aptitudes or dispositions, the teaching task is to move the learner toward a desired outcome. Selecting the best means by which to move forward depends, at least in part, on having an understanding of the present location, interests and needs of the learner. The needs of learners, which must be divined through experience or determined through investigation and trialing, are influenced among other things by the likely:

- conditions of the student's place of study;
- student's time availability;
- range and levels of existing knowledge and skills of students;
- alternative conceptualizations of a phenomenon entertained by students, both initially and as they progress.

Creating an appropriate learning environment may be assisted in the development of learning materials by:

- calling upon instructional designers as well as expert teachers in the design of learning materials;
- careful trialing of materials during the design and development phases.

Investigating and responding to learner needs and preferences has cost implications. As we explained in Chapter 4, attempting to contain teacher–learner interaction requires greater investment in design and development if quality is to be maintained. The point at which the investment in design and development of courseware is economical is discussed in Chapter 5. Suffice to say here it is easy to underestimate the complexity of effective design and development.

Roles in design and development of courseware

If you determine that courseware will be designed and developed in-house, then decisions need to be made about design and development responsibilities. Individuals teaching in a face-to-face environment often complement their teaching with digital technologies and some will have the necessary expertise to design and develop their own materials. Even in the face-to-face environment, however, teachers typically need assistance with audio and video production and the development of computer-based materials beyond basic presentation materials such as 'Powerpoint' slides. One approach is to provide in-service training to teachers to allow them to take a 'do-it-yourself' approach. Another is to provide support.

In-service training, or recruiting teachers with knowledge and skills in the design and development of digital learning materials, has advantages and limitations.

Adopting a multi-skilling approach

Some education and training institutions are putting considerable effort into enhancing the technical skills and knowledge of their teaching staff to allow them to engage directly in digital media design, development and production rather than relying upon the services of instructional designers and media producers and technicians.

The advantages of multi-skilling teachers include:

- The borderlines between the technological and the learning aspects of new learning technologies are difficult to define and it could be argued that their separation is theoretically unsound – the technologies constitute an integral part of the learners' experience; they are part of the learning plan and part of the educational precinct.
- Teachers remain central to and in control of teaching and learning transactions, which may enhance communication in the educational process.
- Teachers understand the education and training objectives for which they are designing.
- Many technological problems can be solved on the spot with suitable development of staff capabilities.
- The possibilities and capacity of technology to contribute to learning is best realized when those responsible for developing learning environments understand the capability of the technologies.
- The teachers are well placed to monitor and evaluate the application of the technology and to modify it to meet changing needs.
- Multi-skilling of the workforce allows greater flexibility in the allocation of time to various tasks and reduces downtime where one skill is not required for a period.

A specialist approach

Specialists who might combine with subject matter experts to develop courseware and related products and services include:

- instructional designers who are experts in education and training approaches and formats which are effective in supporting independent learning;
- computer technicians;
- multimedia programmers, expert in programming computers to produce multimedia effects or in utilizing multimedia authoring software;
- computer technicians who have knowledge and skills in the operation and maintenance of information technology hardware and software;
- audiovisual media technicians who have knowledge and skills in the operation

and maintenance of audiovisual equipment (though with the convergence of audiovisual and computing media the boundary between computer and audiovisual technicians is blurring);

- audiovisual media producers who assist in scripting audiovisual sequences and in directing and editing audiovisual productions;
- graphic designers who are experts in the design of computer and visual graphics and in the presentation of materials;
- photographers who are experts in image capture, digital manipulation and presentation;
- desktop publishers who are experts in the design and production of print-based and screen-based presentation of materials.

Instructional design requires special mention as it is sometimes seen as within the realm or expertise of teachers. Educational providers with a history in distance education and flexible delivery engage instructional designers. There is a developed body of understanding about effective support of learning at a distance. This includes means of clarifying objectives or desired learning outcomes; the analysis and structuring of subject matter; the prediction of user responses to material presented and the adaptation of materials design accordingly; and the integration of assessment and the provision of feedback. Instructional designers come from an understanding of learning usually based on a consistent theoretical position. In post-secondary education where teachers are employed for their understanding of the subject area rather than their knowledge of learning theory or their ability to teach, the potential for appropriate instructional design to make a difference to learning outcomes is great, particularly where the student is remote from the teacher. Processes engaged in by instructional designers, from clarifying objectives through to devising assessment and feedback mechanisms, might be applied to advantage in any teaching situation, but the systematic approach adopted is critical the more flexible the form of delivery. There is a risk that courseware designed by subject specialists will be more concerned with what the teacher presents than with how the student is required to behave or is likely to behave when undertaking the subject.

The advantages of a specialist approach are that:

- Technical problems are resolved effectively.
- Specialists appreciate the technical capabilities and application possibilities of the digital technologies.
- Specialists keep the organization abreast of the latest technological developments.
- Teachers may lack instructional design expertise for non–face-to-face educational interactions. Instructional design for courseware is an expert process.
- Courseware development can be a tedious business with a small element of a program needing to be trialed many times before a product is released. The process may be more attenuated with lack of design and development expertise. The cost relativities of teachers, programmers, graphic artists, video producers and video technicians need to be considered.

- The professional life of teachers and trainers is often already multifaceted, including research and administrative responsibilities and other workplace requirements.

In general terms, it would be unreasonable to expect teaching staff to have a high level of understanding and skill in information systems and their operation and maintenance. Neither can they be expected to have expertise in programming for digital media; in the operation and maintenance of audiovisual equipment; in scripting audiovisual sequences and in directing and editing audiovisual productions; in design of computer and visual graphics and in presentation of materials; in image capture and manipulation; and in the design and production of print-based and screen-based presentation of materials.

In making a decision on whether to adopt a specialist approach you need to take into account the size of your enterprise and the consequent scope for specialization. An organization engaging in digital delivery on a large scale may be able to support specialists in each of the technical areas. If a specialist approach is used, not only are the costs of initial training much reduced, but the costs of keeping skills current are also reduced. Furthermore, fewer software licences and less equipment are required. You need, however, to determine the range of specialists who will be engaged on an ongoing basis and where expertise will be brought in as required.

For smaller providers a limited range of specialist technical services may be provided with other areas bought-in on occasion, contracted out, incorporated in the roles of teachers, or not provided. As indicated in Chapter 7 (see Figure 7.1) the zones of expertise of staff are nominal rather than discrete. Some areas of technical expertise are more aligned with usual teaching activities than others and may be more readily taken up by teaching staff than is the case for other technical functions. Various specializations might be combined in one staff member and with the convergence of audiovisual and computing technologies this is more likely to apply in future.

When using specialists, we advocate the use of a team approach to courseware design and development. The team approach was pioneered by the UK Open University and is now used widely within distance education.

Should technical experts be employed or hired in?

Design and development in-house may involve buying-in expertise on a consultancy or short-term employment basis. Buying-in expertise has a 'just-in-time' logic that allows educational providers to acquire the quality and quantity of expertise required when needed without employing unnecessary labour. There can, however, be disadvantages:

- The ownership of intellectual property in courseware can be confused by the use of consultants (see Chapter 4).
- Courseware design and development is seldom a one-up process. Trialing is necessary; unexpected glitches occur over time; material requires updating

or elaboration; and teaching staff and students continually desire improvements. If understanding of the programming of the courseware walks out the door with the consultant or short-term employee, amendments may be difficult or impractical.

- Corporate memory depends in part on retaining expertise in courseware design and development.

With regard to the last point, corporate memory can be enhanced by organized approaches to observing and documenting design and development processes and by evaluation during the design and development phases of a courseware project as well as upon completion. A systematic approach to the construction of corporate memory may help to offset the transitory nature of expertise obtained from consultants and short-term employees.

Courseware may be developed within a software development package or an integrated electronic learning environment obtainable on the market. Courseware development packages include Toolbook and MacroMedia Director, which automate elements of courseware programming. The software packages require some training to operate them. The packages can be used by teachers but teachers may need the support of instructional designers, graphics artists, video producers and other technicians.

The collaborative approach

If you want to target a field of study that is also being targeted by other providers you may find it worthwhile entering into collaboration with one or more other providers as a way of reducing the level of your investment in design and development through sharing the costs. Laurillard argues that the high cost of producing good quality multimedia material makes it impractical for most institutions to design and develop their own courseware (Laurillard, 1993).

Competitive considerations may discourage you from collaborating but collaboration can coexist with competition. As the knowledge media breaks down barriers of distance, the number of competitors will increase. One may choose to collaborate with some providers while competing with others. Joint ventures are standard practice in the world of business and will become increasingly more common in education and training.

Potential clients may be inclined to select professionally designed and developed courseware, which suggests that providers who have small-scale operations in the particular area may need to collaborate with at least some of their potential competitors to produce a high quality product. Potential clients may choose courseware according to the reputation and prestige of the provider. Who will want to take a course from an obscure provider when digital technology allows them to take a course from a prestigious institution? Collaboration between providers may seek to address the marketability of courseware as much as the logistics and the costs of design and development.

The range of organizations with which you might collaborate need not be limited to other education or training providers. Potential collaborators also include marketing or financial organizations, or organizations that have a training need of their own in the area you want to target.

Summary

Digital media can be used to provide self-contained learning packages, systems for communication between learners and those who can assist their learning, or some combination of these. A combination will usually be appropriate. While self-contained packages provide for time, pace and place flexibility, they have limited capacity to respond to individual needs and they are expensive to design and develop. Approaches based on computer-mediated communication, on the other hand, are expensive to operate and generally need to be supplemented by other learning resources.

Education and training providers wishing to employ new knowledge media have a choice between designing and developing their own courseware, utilizing available courseware, or collaborating with others in the design and development or in the purchase of courseware. The appropriate line of action depends among other things upon the size of the market or user group, the peculiarity of the course and the shelf-life of materials.

In choosing to use available software there are a number of considerations that might be taken into account. These include responsiveness to user requirements; the purpose for which the courseware is designed; prerequisite skills and knowledge; the appropriateness of materials; the learning strategies employed; the user-friendliness of materials; the support services available; and cost-effectiveness.

Where the design path is taken a choice needs to be made between buying in expert help and doing the job in-house. An alternative to designing and developing your own courseware is to collaborate with other organizations. Collaboration may be between providers or with other enterprises. Such collaboration may include educational institutions, workplace training providers, and enterprises that specialize in digital technology and/or marketing and financial institutions.

Chapter 9

Redesigning learner support services

In this chapter we examine the ways in which the support services provided to students can be translated into an electronic environment. The support services we examine are:

- help-desk services for handling academic and administrative inquiries;
- library services;
- counselling services.

Setting up help-desk services

When we examined the factors that governed the costs of electronic delivery in Chapter 4, we pointed out that one-to-one communication with students represents a variable cost that has the potential to escalate the cost per student of delivering distance education programmes. We indicated that for delivery costs to be contained, it is here that savings need to be found.

One way in which this can be achieved is by making courseware as self-contained as possible. It is always desirable to trial the use of courseware during development by using as diverse a sample of students as practicable in order that the types of problems students are likely to encounter can be anticipated in advance. Nevertheless, even when there has been conscientious attention to detail in the development of learning packages, students will still discover that they are missing important information, or that they have questions related to administrative matters or to the content of their courses.

A second strategy is to provide students with easy to use ways of obtaining information themselves. 'Frequently asked questions', bulletin boards and class conferences enable students to obtain answers to commonly asked questions quickly and easily. Yet there will be some students who have a low tolerance for searching out their own answers, and there will be some problems students encounter that require recourse to an academic or administrative adviser as the only way to obtain an answer.

Inability to obtain satisfactory answers to queries promptly is known to be one of the factors that leads to students dropping out of distance education programmes.

Major distance education providers generally find that the majority of student queries that originate from students relate to administrative issues, such as changes of address, examination arrangements and missing course material. It is possible to make considerable savings in labour costs by filtering student requests for assistance so that they are directed to those who are best able to handle them. This approach can also reduce the turnaround time for inquiries. By adopting this approach, only education and training issues reach the teacher. Filtering messages requires setting up a central point of contact for student queries.

Setting up a central communication node

The establishment of a central contact point for telephone and e-mail messages is a strategy commonly used by distance education centres to ensure that students have their queries handled promptly. However, this type of service can be implemented even more efficiently and effectively in an online environment because it is possible for the logging and tracking functions to be combined with the messaging function.

One major advantage of routing all inquiries to a central point is that the service can provide responses out of hours – at times when mature students can be contacted and when they generally do most of their studying. Another advantage is that inquiries can be logged and tracked. If a faculty member is attending a conference or is absent through illness, student inquiries are still answered. In these situations, a student's query can be diverted to the next most suitable person for an answer.

Filtering can also be used for academic inquiries. Again, this can be facilitated by online communications. If learners are encouraged in the first instance to contact other learners through e-mail and electronic discussion and chat mechanisms, a teacher will only need to step in where discussion is going off track or coming to a halt. A teacher may also prepare responses to frequently asked questions and distribute them as requested or through an electronic bulletin board.

Choosing software systems to support help-desk functions

It is possible for a help-desk service to be based on commercially available groupware software or to be integrated into the electronic learning environment. However, it is likely that a more efficient service can be provided by customizing the support software or developing a dedicated system that operates in a way that recognizes the standard practices and divisions of responsibility within the organization.

Putting library services online

How important are library services to distance learners?

The need that distance learners have for library services will depend on the nature of their studies and also on the manner in which the programme on which they are enrolled is being delivered.

Technical and vocational education programmes generally do not make extensive use of primary sources. Libraries are used to provide access to textbooks and other resource material such as video and audio tapes. Learning packages that are produced for students studying at this level are typically designed to be fully self-contained.

In higher education, students are expected to learn to make use of the literature of their discipline. Most courses require students to draw on primary sources. However, that does not necessarily involve making use of library collections. Because of the delays that occur in the turnaround of library materials, the limited availability of library resources and the limited time that students have in which to complete the requirements of most subjects, most distance education providers have steered away from reliance on library collections.

If the class size is sufficiently large, a university may find it practicable to publish readers which students purchase in the same way as they purchase textbooks. However, the most common arrangement is that students are provided with photocopies of original material under the 'fair dealing' clauses of copyright legislation. In the case of institutions that supply students with fully self-contained learning packages, students tend not to make use of the borrowing service.

At the postgraduate level, access to primary sources is an intrinsic part of students' studies. In a recent survey of 1,000 postgraduate students across 19 disciplines in 23 universities in the UK, 78 per cent of respondents said that they felt the need for supplementary reading material. However, 51 per cent said that making use of library resources was not explicitly required of them (Stephens *et al.*, 1997).

Inclusion of copies of primary source material in learning packages has been a pragmatic response to the difficulty faced by the distance learner in obtaining access to such material. However, this expedient conflicts with the strongly espoused principle that a university education should encourage students to become autonomous learners. Many distance educators fear that electronic delivery will push distance education further in the direction of pre-packaged learning. However, Stephens *et al.* (1997) believe that collaboration between teachers and librarians will expand the boundaries of distance learning.

How much scholarly literature is now available online?

In a course that is being delivered online, primary and secondary source material should ideally be accessible online. Technically, there is no reason why this should not be the case. In reality, only a small fraction of published literature can presently be accessed in this way. The reason is largely commercial. Publishers are still grappling with the issue of devising a business model for marketing scholarly journals and other literature electronically. Some progress has been made. A number of publishers will now supply academic libraries with journals in either print or machine-readable form. However, the subscription arrangements for online versions of scholarly journals do not yet take into account the changing access patterns – for example, the fact that a student may be located in a different country from the institution at which they are enrolled.

Non-commercial publishers of scholarly journals tend to be less concerned with profitability than with access. They are therefore moving more quickly than commercial publishers to online distribution. For them, such a move reduces costs and decreases the labour of distribution.

There is also a proliferation of new electronic journals. For example, the *Journal of Asynchronous Learning* is available online and can be downloaded at no cost. Print copies may also be purchased at a price comparable to print-only journals.

In addition to the scholarly journals that are now available on the Web, there is a growing volume of authoritative information originating directly from government and semi-government organizations, research organizations and universities. It is becoming increasingly common to find academic staff using the Web to publicize the results of their work by placing their publications on the Web, where they are not precluded from doing so by copyright restrictions. However, monographs and most reference sources are still not available online. For these types of resources alternative methods of delivery are needed.

How practicable is it to use electronic document delivery?

Given this situation, the challenge for distance education providers moving into online delivery is to find the optimal combination of services for supporting students, taking into account copyright restrictions and the limitations imposed by technology. There is no reason why the arrangements that have operated for print delivery cannot be extended to students studying online.

For undergraduate courses, the most convenient method of offering original source material online is through an electronic reserve collection. Schiller and Cunningham (1998) have provided detailed statistics on a pilot project in which an electronic reserve collection was operated across several campuses of the State University of New York. Documents were scanned, converted to either portable document format (PDF) or HTML and then linked to the library Web site. They found that it was possible to provide this type of service more efficiently by encoding documents in PDF rather than HTML. PDF offered several other advantages as well:

- PDF format retains the original layout – important when documents contain tables – yet documents can still be searched by keyword and given hypertext links;
- PDF documents can be given individual passwords;
- high-speed scanners that are capable of encoding documents in PDF are now available.

Copyright legislation differs from country to country. However, provision usually exists for 'fair use' for a range of purposes including scholarship and research. The 'fair use' provisions of copyright legislation may allow libraries to establish electronic reserve collections under similar arrangements to those which libraries must adhere to in photocopying material to hold in a physical reserve collection. While individual situations should be checked, in countries where such copying is permissible the conditions under which such copying is allowed are generally that the amount of material being copied is no more than one article in a journal or one chapter in a book and that the document carries an appropriate copyright notice. The circumstances under which permission usually needs to be sought include:

- when more than one article from a journal or one chapter from a book is needed for electronic reserve;
- when an item is needed for two or more consecutive course offer periods;
- when a charge is being made for access which exceeds the distribution costs.

If these criteria cannot be met, then clearance needs to be sought from the copyright owner, who may require the payment of a fee.

Universities that have not hitherto had much experience in the large-scale provision of print-based distance education may consider the requirements for copyright clearance quite onerous. However, major distance education providers recognize this to be one of the routine functions of distance education delivery. The key to managing this function efficiently is to develop a streamlined set of procedures for locating the owners of copyright material, requesting clearance and negotiating usage fees.

Inter-library loan agreements permit libraries to make copies of limited amounts of copyright material for research and study. The provisions of these agreements allow this service to be extended to students studying online. Under the fair dealing provisions of copyright legislation, there is generally scope to charge students for delivery of electronic copies of copyright material provided that the charge levied does not exceed the cost of providing the service.

The greatest difficulty here is that the library system is not set up to offer this type of service on a large scale. The inter-library loans services are generally set up to provide copies of journal articles and book chapters to a small academic research community. They are not equipped or staffed to provide electronic copies to a much larger student community.

An alternative means of providing a document delivery service online is to become a subscriber to the UnCover service operated internationally by the

Colorado Alliance of University Libraries (CARL). This provides fax delivery of articles from a collection of over 17,000 journals. The response time is generally less than 24 hours and users can search the database of articles via the Web <http://uncwb.carl.org>. UnCover takes care of copyright fees and the cost of retrieving an article via UnCover is made up of a standard document delivery charge plus a variable copyright charge.

The changing role of academic libraries

In considering how library services might best be provided to students studying online, it is important to take account of the impact on the role of academic libraries of changes in the way information is being located. Whereas the traditional library has been seen as the repository of print materials, in an online environment it is possible to go directly to the original source of a document.

The professional of the future will increasingly go directly to the Internet as the first method of tracking down information. Students need to be trained to become proficient users of Internet-based information retrieval tools and to discriminate between authoritative information and information of questionable value.

In this changing environment, the role of libraries is changing too. Rather than serving as custodians of information resources, librarians are increasingly taking on the role of guides to the world of information.

Library services are serving a more important educative function. For the learner studying at a distance, the type of service that is generally most useful is being able to obtain information on what resources are available on a particular topic and where to find them. The Internet Public Library (http://www.ipl.org) provides a model of the type of library needed by the online learner.

Notwithstanding the limited availability of online resources there are nevertheless a large number of ways in which academic libraries can take advantage of the Internet to assist online learners to obtain better access to information resources. These include:

- providing online access to catalogues and indexes;
- publishing an online set of guides to information services and sources;
- establishing an electronic reserve collection for distribution of reference materials;
- enabling students to make borrowing requests online;
- providing access to subscription journals available online;
- conducting online classes on accessing resources on the Internet;
- providing advice to students via e-mail and asynchronous conferences on how to access Internet resources;
- establishing cooperative arrangements with other academic libraries to enable distance learners to access print holdings;
- providing online advice to students on the availability of print resources at nearby local academic libraries.

Offering counselling services online

Student counselling services generally conceive of their responsibilities as extending across three main areas:

- provision of counselling in relation to personal issues;
- assisting students to develop their social networks;
- provision of careers and learning skills advice.

Advising on personal issues

It is usual for counselling services to provide a range of free literature on topics such as health and students' rights and responsibilities. Most counselling services have recognized the potential that the Web offers for making this type of literature more readily available. Once this type of literature has been placed on the Web it is accessible to students, irrespective of the mode or place of study.

If students are only able to access this type of literature online, they may need to be alerted to its availability. It will be advisable to provide pointers to the literature from locations where students are given directions on the course requirements.

Student counsellors are accustomed to providing face-to-face consultations to students who seek assistance with personal issues. Non-verbal cues are often of critical importance in personal counselling. Computer-mediated communication is a much less satisfactory means of offering this type of assistance than face-to-face consultations, but it is still able to play a role. Counselling staff who have not had previous experience in online counselling should be given training in the characteristics of computer-mediated communication before being asked to attempt to use it in this way.

One way in which institutions can discharge their responsibilities to students in relation to counselling on personal issues is by entering into cooperative arrangements with the counselling services of other institutions.

Assisting students to develop social networks

The sense of isolation that many students studying at a distance experience has been one of the recurrent themes in the distance education literature. Asynchronous conferencing and chat systems offer the means of breaking down this sense of isolation. Providing the facilities for computer-mediated communication is an essential prerequisite to enabling students to meet in virtual venues. Incorporating virtual meeting places specifically for social interaction into the design of online learning environments is therefore as important as providing student lounges and cafes in an on-campus environment. However, just as 'ice breaker' activities are often needed to enable some students to feel comfortable in interacting in face-to-face situations, structured activities may be needed to enable some students to feel comfortable in interacting online.

Providing careers and learning skills counselling

Careers counselling includes providing advice on career options as well as on study pathways. Given the types of students who presently choose to study at a distance and the types of students who are most likely to be attracted to online learning, it is probable that the provision of advice on course choice will best meet students' needs if information is organized by fields of study rather than by institution. National and international directories of courses, particularly if they are cross-referenced with occupational information, are likely to be more useful in locating suitable courses of study than catalogues of the offerings of individual providers.

May (1998) has reviewed the range of sources of career information on the Internet to assist career counsellors and their clients in investigating career choices. He identifies Richard Bolles' *What color is your parachute? The Net Guide* (http://www.washingtonpost.com/parachute) and *The Riley Guide* (http://www.jobtrak.com/jobguide) as two of the most useful Web sites providing meta-listings of online careers resources.

While most universities are now using the World Wide Web to make information on their range of courses available over the Internet, comparatively little consideration is currently being given to the way in which information needs to be structured and presented for accessibility. Phillips *et al.* (1998) describe the way in which the UK Open University is seeking to present itself to prospective students and to support actual students in making their course choices.

Summary

Delivering courses online at a distance calls for a reorganization of the ways in which support services are provided. This is important both to ensure that the highest standard of support is provided for the resources available as well as to avoid the possibility of costs escalating. In most situations the most cost-effective arrangement will be achieved through establishing a centralized 'help-desk' facility to track and manage students' requests for assistance, to direct queries to the staff who are best placed to answer them and to ensure that requests for assistance receive timely replies.

The extent to which it is possible to provide library services online is presently constrained by copyright restrictions and the high cost of subscriptions to the electronic versions of commercially published journals. However, the use of electronic reserve collections and electronic delivery copies of articles through the inter-library loans arrangements allows considerable scope for development of an online service. Moreover the growth of electronic journals and other Internet-published literature will steadily reduce the reliance of academic programmes on print literature.

In designing library services it is important to take into account the changing patterns of use of information retrieval systems resulting from the growth of the

Internet and the World Wide Web. The types of library services that students are likely to need most in future are those that direct them to available Internet resources and train them in the use of Internet-based information retrieval rather than simply the loan of monographs and the copying of articles.

Counselling services need to place their print literature on the Web, if they have not already done so. The major challenge for counselling services will be to test the limits of the electronic media for one-to-one counselling.

Chapter 10

Developing an evaluation strategy

In this chapter we first identify the object of evaluation where knowledge media is employed and some of the issues involved in evaluating. We focus particularly on teaching and learning innovations or projects utilizing knowledge media. We look at what you evaluate, when you evaluate, how you evaluate, how you interpret the results of evaluation, and who should evaluate. We then go on in more detail to discuss criteria for evaluating learning with knowledge media. We offer a frame of reference for selecting criteria and demonstrate how it might be employed.

Evaluation and the knowledge media

In the quest to improve access, to reduce costs and to improve the quality of education and training, evaluation plays a vital role. New educational technologies, along with new uses of existing ones, are being employed to improve both access and quality. Effort is being put into projects that use knowledge media to supplement or replace face-to-face classroom tuition and to facilitate distance learning.

Are the anticipated benefits realized and are the benefits worth the effort? Systematic evaluation can help answer this question.

Evaluation of knowledge media initiatives cannot only assess and place value upon the outcomes of projects employing media but, if applied to the early stages of initiatives, can help to shape them and improve the chances of producing outcomes that are valued.

The use of knowledge media is often evaluated against objectives of projects involving new educational technologies or against alternative approaches. In either of these cases the evaluation is of the use of media over a contained period. For this reason we will focus in this chapter on evaluating projects or initiatives employing the knowledge media which have a beginning, a development phase and an outcome. This raises a number of issues and challenges, some of which relate to the nature of learning through the use of digital technology and some of which derive from focusing on innovations.

Some issues arising from the nature of the knowledge media

The use of knowledge media for delivery of a course implies that something more than human resources of speech and action are used to facilitate learning. That something might be CD-based multimedia, Web resources retrieved from the Internet, a computer-aided learning program or a computer-managed learning system. These media may be used with stand-alone delivery packages or used in conjunction with teacher–student interactions – whether face-to-face or at a distance. In evaluating the use of new educational technologies it is important to encompass both where it is employed to deliver stand-alone resources and where it is used in teacher–student and student–student interaction.

Learning through knowledge media, then, is not a discretely definable process. There are many forms of media and many strategies for their use. This means that the knowledge media *per se* are not readily evaluated. All that can be evaluated are particular teaching and learning activities that involve the use of some form of digital technology.

The use of knowledge media to facilitate learning does not imply that the learning take any particular form. The learning may involve acquiring information, understanding, skills, competencies and dispositions. Likewise, the learning acquired through digital technology may be assessed or evidenced through processes requiring recall, analysis, synthesizing, hypothesizing or competent or creative behaviours. What is being evaluated, then, is not a particular form of learning.

Neither does the use of knowledge media in itself imply a particular learning process informed by a particular learning theory. The process could involve simple teacher–driven instruction. It may involve design catering for graded or alternative conceptualizations. The student may be largely passive or active and learning may take place through discovery or through direct instruction. The design of learning materials may be based on behaviourist, information processing, cognitive, humanistic or constructivist theories.

What is being evaluated then is not a particular approach to learning informed by a particular learning theory generic to the use of knowledge media. What is available for evaluation is particular education and training initiatives or innovations that employ new educational technologies.

Some issues arising from focusing on innovations

What constitutes an innovation? We need to decide how innovative an innovation has to be in order to serve as an indication of the value of adopting knowledge media for education or training purposes.

Use of instructional technologies can be more or less innovative. They can be innovative in some contexts while established in others. In trying to evaluate the impact of innovation using knowledge media do we include new uses of old technology such as television or just new technologies? Do we include innovations employing relatively low-tech media, such as e-mail, as well as high-tech multimedia? You need to define the boundaries of the types of innovation according to your own context and purposes.

How can we make evaluation of knowledge media effective?

The value that the knowledge media contributes to improved access, quality and efficiency is still being contested. Many innovations involving knowledge media have not been appropriately evaluated. Many have not been evaluated at all. Often evaluations of educational innovations involving digital technology originate from the innovators themselves. We can attend to the first point raised here – the want of systematic evaluation. We can also attend to the second point – evaluation by interested parties, in the sense that we can seek independent evaluation of knowledge media.

We cannot avoid the fact that evaluation is subjective. Evaluation involves placing a value upon findings. We may seek to make the data gathering as objective as possible. Yet the questions to be investigated, the choice of data to be gathered, the acceptance and rejection of data, the meaning of the findings and the reporting of them, are bound to reflect some subjectivity. It involves selection and judgement which depend on the context of the evaluation, the interests of the evaluator and the frames of reference chosen by the evaluator for selecting evaluation criteria. As a consequence, one person's evaluation may not be suitable for another person's decision making.

Some key issues in undertaking evaluation

The obvious value of evaluation of knowledge media projects is as an aid to decision making. What is less obvious is:

- what to evaluate;
- when to evaluate;
- how to evaluate;
- who should evaluate.

Let us examine each of these points in turn.

What to evaluate

We cannot evaluate the knowledge media as such any more than we could evaluate print, or evaluate the overhead projector. Evaluation of particular media is sometimes attempted. It produces results by media type, for example that overhead projectors are valuable for information presentation. But with some creativity, we could use an overhead projector to silhouette glove puppets in a role-play. We certainly cannot evaluate the computer as a medium when it may be used in more ways than we could define. The value of a medium depends on how it is used. We can, therefore, evaluate media only in the context of their use. For this reason we focus in this chapter on evaluating projects involving new educational technologies.

When to evaluate

It is traditional to distinguish between formative and summative evaluation. Summative evaluation is evaluation at the conclusion of a project. Formative evaluation is evaluation conducted during a project.

Formative evaluation is undertaken during a project in order to monitor progress and modify developments in the project as it proceeds. Formative evaluation might be undertaken at the end of discrete phases of the project. It might take the form of evaluating components of a project as they are developed or trialing a pilot version of a project.

Summative evaluation is suitable for reflecting upon the success of a project. It might be undertaken in order to satisfy accountability requirements established by sponsors of an innovation or project. Summative evaluation can be used to determine appropriate applications of the product and any support or supplementary materials or services that may be necessary. Summative evaluation can inform decisions concerning similar projects in the future. As summative evaluation usually comes at the end of a project, it is not able to inform developments during that particular project. Figure 10.1 illustrates the relationship between the timing of formative and summative evaluation.

Two further types of evaluation may also be employed: design evaluation and an evaluation of needs or a needs analysis.

Design evaluation, like formative evaluation, is undertaken during a project to influence developments. However, whereas formative evaluation relates to phases or elements of a project as they are completed, design evaluation relates to stages or elements of a project yet to be commenced. Design evaluation can address minor points such as the way that people are likely to interpret an icon on a screen, or it can address more fundamental matters. For instance, suppose that it was proposed to design a sequence in a multimedia program in which students make a choice on the basis that they are able to distinguish the graph of an exponential function from the graph of a simple curve. It would be worth finding out whether students of the type likely to use the product are able to make this distinction. Design evaluation can be critical in major multimedia projects. It

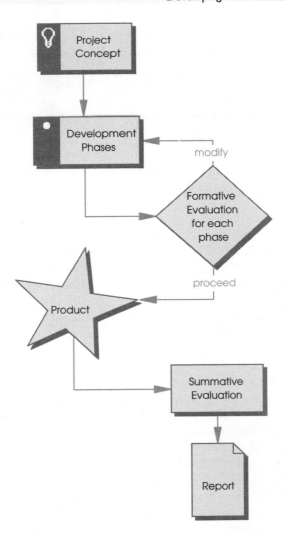

Figure 10.1 *A simple evaluation model*

can uncover faulty assumptions about the capabilities, interests and predilections of users that could lead to investment in a design that later needs to be modified or even abandoned.

Whereas formative and summative evaluation may be undertaken as a matter of course, design evaluation requires recognition of a need to check assumptions on which proposed developments are based. A project coordinator needs to continually scan design proposals, identifying underlying assumptions that need testing.

Evaluation of needs is the first step in the process of mounting a project employing new educational technologies. This type of evaluation asks questions such as:

- What education or training need or needs is the project intended to serve?
- Who are the intended users?
- Is there a genuine demand?
- Are the needs those which have been anticipated or should the original concept be modified?
- Are the proposed users, or someone on their behalf, prepared to meet the design, development, production and marketing cost of the project?

The last question may be seen as a further form of evaluation – a market analysis.

Figure 10.2 illustrates a more sophisticated evaluation model than that in Figure 10.1. It incorporates evaluation of needs, a market analysis and design evaluation.

Whether we choose to use a simple model which involves only formative and summative evaluation or a more sophisticated model, evaluation should not be an add-on or an afterthought. Evaluation needs to be planned into a project from the time it is conceived. The evaluation of needs, and a market evaluation if appropriate, should occur prior to the design of a knowledge media project. Design evaluation needs to take place prior to the commencement of development of materials and may need to be carried out several times as development proceeds from one phase to the next. Formative evaluation likewise needs to occur at any stage a discrete element of the project is developed.

How to evaluate

What should we look for in instruments for conducting an evaluation? While evaluation is necessarily subjective, we can aim to make the means of gathering evaluation data valid and reliable.

Validity refers to the extent to which an evaluation instrument measures what is intended to be measured. Validity can be improved by carefully considering what is to be observed and by carefully crafting questions for checklists or interviews. For example, if we wish to discover whether potential students are likely to enrol in a unit using knowledge media, then piloting the unit and asking whether students enjoyed using the particular medium does not ask the right question, at least not on its own. It is a question people typically include in evaluation of knowledge media but, in this case, it is not what you are setting out to test. It would be more pertinent to ask students whether, based on their experience with the pilot, they would enrol in such a unit in future.

Reliability refers to the capacity of the instrument to return results that are consistent and that will be interpreted consistently. Reliability is indicated where there is minimal scope for argument about the meaning of questions asked or checklists employed or about the meaning of results. This could be achieved, for instance, by using several investigators who agree on guidelines to be used for interpreting data gathered from a questionnaire or by having the records of an interview and its interpretation confirmed by interviewees.

It is sometimes necessary to accept a trade off between validity and reliability. You can increase reliability by asking yes/no questions on a questionnaire so

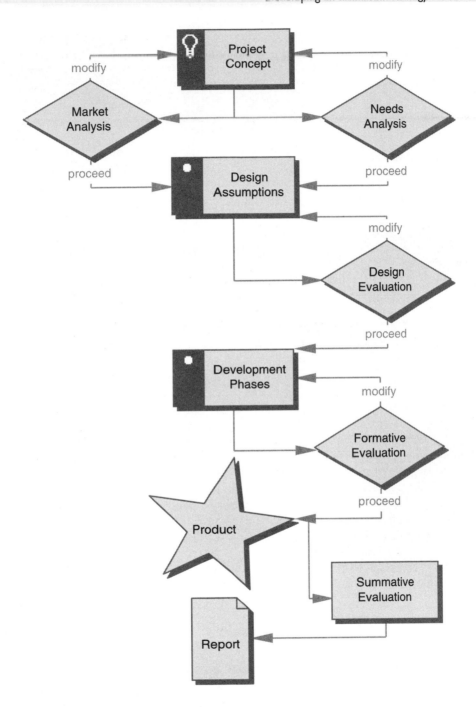

Figure 10.2 *A pre- and post-development evaluation model*

that it could be read by multiple investigators or by a computer and produce the same result. However, in switching to that approach you may impair the validity of the results. The evaluation instrument may give little scope for reporting unexpected or complex responses to the educational initiative being investigated – that is it may fail to produce a complete picture of responses and in that sense lack validity.

Who should evaluate

Applications for funding for innovative educational projects generally require a description of the evaluation strategy that will be used. This opens up the possibility that evaluation is left in the hands of those undertaking the project. There are two questions you might consider: should evaluation be in the hands of an expert evaluator and should the evaluator be independent of the project team?

With regard to expertise, drafting an evaluation plan for a project requires some understanding of the nature of the process, of the phases and forms of evaluation, and of the design of instruments that optimize validity and reliability in data collection. You may have access to expert evaluators. On the other hand you might acquire appropriate expertise through using reference material such as this chapter, or evaluation texts, or by having staff undertake professional development programmes in evaluation.

There are advantages in having an independent evaluator undertake some forms of evaluation while having those involved in a project conduct other forms of evaluation. A market analysis might best be performed by a person independent of a proposed project to determine whether, from a sponsor's point of view, it is worth proceeding and the nature of what is demanded. Needs analysis, design evaluations and formative evaluations, on the other hand, are generally best carried out by those involved. These forms of evaluation inform design and development of the project. Various parties have an interest in summative evaluation – sponsors of projects, users of innovations as well those immediately involved in the project. As a result there is an advantage in having someone independent of the project carry out summative evaluation.

The remainder of this chapter provides some guidance for the conduct of project evaluations. It is intended to inform and support both evaluation under-taken by members of a project team and independent evaluation conducted by people lacking evaluation expertise.

Some guidelines for carrying out evaluation

Evaluation instruments

There are many types of instruments or means of evaluation that can be applied to the use of courseware based on knowledge media or to the use of knowledge media in delivery. The instruments most commonly used are:

- expert reviews;
- surveys;
- observations.

For an expert review of the product or service a report is obtained from an appropriate expert. There are at least three forms of expertise that are pertinent to this type of evaluation: subject matter expertise, instructional design expertise and media expertise. It may be considered important in a particular situation to call on a variety of experts. When this approach is used, the sponsor of the evaluation usually hands over the responsibility for selecting the criteria for evaluation to the expert.

A survey instrument such as a questionnaire may be devised to evaluate an educational product or service. Decisions have to be made about criteria for selecting items to include. Decisions also have to be made about how open-ended the questions should be. (These points are discussed later.)

Observation may be made of the product or service in action, possibly against a checklist. The process might involve discussion with users as they employ the knowledge media. Videotaping use of the product or service can assist in making a detailed analysis of user behaviours. Again criteria for establishing a checklist or items to be observed and for their interpretation have to be determined. (See the section on criteria below.)

Selecting an appropriate survey instrument

Questionnaires, interview schedules and checklists may be used as evaluation instruments in a number of approaches. Is there an appropriate format for such instruments? Should they adopt closed formats such as yes/no, Likert scales (ie, strongly agree/agree/disagree/strongly disagree) or multiple-choice questions? Should they adopt open formats such as short answer questions, open-ended questions or loosely structured interview schedules? There are a number of considerations in determining whether to evaluate using open or closed forms, including:

- breadth of response versus ease of analysis;
- subjectivity;
- logistics;
- forms of analysis and representation of the data.

Breadth of response versus ease of analysis

Open-ended forms of investigation, such as loosely structured interviews with users or open-ended questions on a questionnaire, allow for unexpected responses and provide for depth of reporting. Closed formats like interviewing against a checklist or multiple-choice questions on a questionnaire make data analysis simpler and more reliable.

Subjectivity

Open forms of data gathering focus the subjectivity at the end of the evaluation, that is in the process of identifying or clustering like responses, in discriminating between responses and in interpreting the findings. Closed forms of investigation focus the subjectivity at the start of the process, that is in determining what questions to ask, in guessing the responses people may wish to make – as in selecting options for multiple-choice questions or bounding the responses people may make as for Likert scales or true/false questions. From this point of view open forms have an advantage. The focus of the subjective element comes after you have heard what respondents have to say rather than before you have heard it.

Logistics

From a logistical point of view open-ended formats require less effort in construction but more in data manipulation and interpretation. Closed formats require more effort in construction, including trialing of questions, but the responses are easy to handle. One consideration here is the scale of the investigation. Designing an elaborate questionnaire makes most sense where the number of people to be surveyed is large. Handling large amounts of qualitative data can be both complex and time-consuming. There are computer programs that assist qualitative data analysis, such as NUD•IST. The programs, however, require some induction and the process of getting the data in a form to optimize the computer analysis takes some time.

Forms of analysis and representation of the data

Closed questionnaires lend themselves to quantitative analysis and reporting. Responses may be presented in the form of graphs and it is possible to execute statistical correlations, for example between demographic elements of the data and successful use of the knowledge media, such as whether males or females, young or old, had most success in using the product. There are a couple of cautions here: the data must be valid in the first place and attaching meaning to the correlations depends on having a theoretical position from which to make an interpretation of any forces at work. It is possible to attach some quantitative elements to open-ended responses, and some qualitative data analysis packages provide this facility, but the quantitative results may well be nonsense. It would be inappropriate to report that 43.36 per cent of respondents said that navigation in the media being investigated was perplexing or confusing when sampling of the population was done on a convenience basis. The reporting implies a level of precision that was not built into the design. Suppose, on the other hand, that this response came from an open-ended question asking what was the most striking impression of the educational media. The fact that navigation was confusing came to mind for nearly half the respondents is much more powerful than 43 per cent of respondents to a closed questionnaire ticking a box which asked if they found the navigation confusing.

Conducting observations of a product or service in action

A product or service resulting from a project may be observed and evaluated against a set of criteria. As indicated in the following section, the criteria may or may not be designed to facilitate comparison with alternative products and services. Where it is designed to be comparative, a quasi-experimental situation can be established to observe the effects of applying the innovation. Comparison may be made with the condition of learners prior to application of the innovation or with a control group.

Some caution should be expressed here. Variables are likely to be very difficult to control or to otherwise account for and there are ethical considerations in experimenting with learners.

To take a quasi-experimental approach requires a theoretical expectation of outcomes and the establishment of an associated hypothesis that can be tested. The selection of an hypothesis often helps to indicate measures that are appropriate, such as observation schedules, pre- and post-tests of knowledge, skills and attitudes, or artefacts produced by the users. It also indicates criteria for judging and interpreting data.

Criteria for evaluating innovations involving knowledge media

Whatever the evaluation instruments and methods we choose to use we need criteria by which to select appropriate questions or matters to evaluate. The brainstorming approach, eg, 'Why don't we ask them whether they found it easy to use?' is sometimes employed. It is inappropriate; it lacks a rationale. There are alternative approaches we can use to establishing criteria by which to evaluate learning that utilizes knowledge media. Four approaches are differentiated here:

- using the objectives of the innovation;
- comparing effectiveness with a previous condition or approach;
- evaluating against the known potential of the technology;
- evaluating against a theoretical position.

A combination of two or more of these approaches is also a possibility. Let us look at each of these approaches in turn.

Goals or objectives-based criteria

If the goals or objectives of the project can be identified, they are frequently used to provide the criteria for evaluation. This approach is satisfactory if the objectives of the particular innovation have been accepted as being worthwhile, if any unanticipated outcomes are seen as irrelevant and if costs are seen as given and acceptable. This is, at least prima facie, the case for some specially funded projects, such as projects funded by a university or by an outside agency which call for submissions for projects meeting certain criteria and provide support to a predetermined level. Even in these situations, evaluating a project against its own objectives is limiting. This method of evaluation will give no indication of unanticipated outcomes that may be as educationally or practically important as the intended outcomes. It does not allow for shifts in objectives. Focusing on project objectives can lead to costs being ignored or at least being taken as given – being those specified in a project submission. In fact there are likely to be costs, both direct and indirect, that were not identified in project submissions. To ignore extraneous benefits, costs and other effects limits the understanding that could inform future actions.

Comparative criteria

An alternative method is to compare the outcomes of an initiative with an approach that does not employ the media innovation. The learning outcomes using the initiation might be compared to learning outcomes using a previous approach, or the learning outcomes for a particular learner might be compared to the condition of the learner prior to using the innovation.

There are two sets of issues in attempting a comparison between teaching approaches: what to keep constant and what additional aspects of the situation need to be examined.

The learning environment is likely to change in multiple ways, so maintaining constants is difficult. If we cannot keep elements of the learning environment constant we could try to run sufficiently extensive trials to use inferential statistics to make comparisons, but this may not be practical either.

It would be unusual for educational and training initiatives using knowledge media to simply change the form of teaching without impacting on other aspects of the educational transaction. The form of learning valued may change, the roles of learners and teachers usually change and even the boundaries of the subject may change. The intended learning outcomes therefore change as do related forms of student assessment. It would not then be appropriate to measure the success of approaches using knowledge media against traditional approaches by using the same test or exam.

The comparative approach, as for other approaches to selecting evaluation criteria, has its limitations but we are often obliged to attempt to answer the question, 'Does the innovation make things better or worse?'. In doing so we need to acknowledge the limitations on our ability to provide a simple answer.

Criteria based on conventional wisdom

A further alternative in establishing criteria is to use benefits and costs anticipated from the literature or experience as a basis for evaluation. The result is to evaluate innovations employing digital technologies against benefits which could, on the basis of conventional wisdom, be expected to flow from them and to likewise evaluate them on the basis of costs which could be expected to be incurred. The rationale for this approach is that it can take into account a wider range of benefits and costs than those identified by the designers of a particular project.

Expectations that arise from conventional wisdom may be that innovations will:

- provide new educational experiences;
- offer greater options for student selection of learning activities;
- extend information resources;
- extend opportunities for exchanges between students and between students and teachers;
- provide better opportunities for monitoring individual student progress;
- provide wider access to learning.

Theoretically-based criteria

This approach to evaluation criteria requires not just a theoretical position on evaluation, but a theoretical position in relation to the realm being evaluated. For example, where learning outcomes are evaluated you need a theoretical understanding of learning processes; where access to education is an issue a position on equity is needed.

To take learning theories as an example, the criteria that one would use to evaluate an education or training innovation would differ according to the understanding of learning held by the evaluator. If you have a behaviourist understanding of learning you might look for a systematic, step-by-step approach, with frequent testing that results in positive or negative reinforcement as appropriate to produce the prescribed learning outcome. An evaluator with a constructivist view of learning might be looking for the opportunity for the learner to engage with the material, bring personal experiences and needs, apply their own meaning and emerge with something applicable to their own situation.

As for any of the approaches to establishing criteria, the theoretical approach has its limitations. It may not address issues of the accountability of innovators to meet agreed objectives; in itself it says nothing about the comparative value of the innovation; and it will not be suitable for a decision maker who holds different ideals or theoretical understandings to those of the evaluator.

Frames of reference for selecting evaluation criteria

A model for selection of evaluation criteria based on the alternative frames of reference outlined above is shown in Figure 10.3.

Combining approaches to establishing criteria

Each of the approaches to establishing evaluation criteria has its use and its limitations. The approaches can be combined. For instance, for accountability purposes one may be obliged to take an objectives-based approach to evaluating an innovation yet still wish to report on unintended outcomes. An electronic training initiative may have been designed to create competency in basic key-boarding but may also have produced some other abilities in the use of software or in the operation or assembly of hardware which could be seen as valuable if criteria beyond the specified objectives were employed.

In combining criteria one has to be clear about the purpose of the evaluation, that is, what things we are putting a value on. These purposes need to be consistent or at least, if they are inconsistent, then the inconsistency needs to be highlighted when reporting. An evaluator coming from a constructivist view of learning who values the opportunity for the learner to engage with the material and to apply their own meaning, may not regard a competency-based learning project as valuable even if it met its declared objectives. You could report on the project from both points of view but the difference in viewpoints needs to be made explicit.

Some good examples of combining criteria based on the educational potential of electronic media with criteria based on theories of learning may be found in the educational literature. Laurillard (1993) adopts expectations of educational media initiatives derived from an intersection of learning theory and an understanding of the potential of various forms of instructional technology. She argues that media should facilitate teaching approaches which are:

- discursive – allowing teachers and students to access each other's conceptions, allowing them to agree goals and allowing students to receive feedback on their actions;
- adaptive – responding to the relationships between teacher and student conceptions;
- interactive – providing meaningful intrinsic feedback to student actions to achieve a task goal;
- reflective – allowing students to link feedback on their actions to the goal.

Educational media can then be evaluated against criteria that:

- emphasize the capacity to describe and re-describe conceptions;
- allow adaptations of task goals, which provide for feedback;
- allow subsequent adaptation of action.

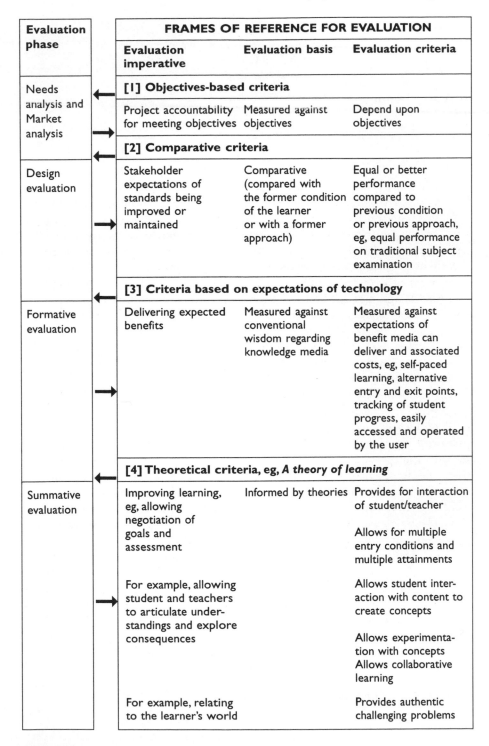

Evaluation phase	FRAMES OF REFERENCE FOR EVALUATION		
	Evaluation imperative	**Evaluation basis**	**Evaluation criteria**
Needs analysis and Market analysis	**[1] Objectives-based criteria**		
	Project accountability for meeting objectives	Measured against objectives	Depend upon objectives
Design evaluation	**[2] Comparative criteria**		
	Stakeholder expectations of standards being improved or maintained	Comparative (compared with the former condition of the learner or with a former approach)	Equal or better performance compared to previous condition or previous approach, eg, equal performance on traditional subject examination
Formative evaluation	**[3] Criteria based on expectations of technology**		
	Delivering expected benefits	Measured against conventional wisdom regarding knowledge media	Measured against expectations of benefit media can deliver and associated costs, eg, self-paced learning, alternative entry and exit points, tracking of student progress, easily accessed and operated by the user
Summative evaluation	**[4] Theoretical criteria, eg, *A theory of learning***		
	Improving learning, eg, allowing negotiation of goals and assessment	Informed by theories	Provides for interaction of student/teacher Allows for multiple entry conditions and multiple attainments
	For example, allowing student and teachers to articulate understandings and explore consequences		Allows student interaction with content to create concepts Allows experimentation with concepts Allows collaborative learning
	For example, relating to the learner's world		Provides authentic challenging problems

Figure 10.3   *A model for selecting criteria for evaluating media innovations*

Table 10.1   *Technology effectiveness framework (Jones et al., 1994)*

	Engaged and sustained learning	Passive learning
High technology	eg, challenging tasks with connectivity	
Low technology		eg, CAL based on drill

Jones *et al.* (1994), drawing on a wide range of writing on learning, establish a 'technology effectiveness framework' (see Table 10.1) setting up quadrants about a learning axis ranging from passive learning (undesirable) to engaged and sustained learning (desirable) and a technology performance axis ranging from low to high. High technology is indicated by: connectivity to resources; inter-connectivity to other participants (teachers or students); inter-operability between systems (eg, the ability to transfer data between systems); distributed resources rather than one source of knowledge (for example extending from stand-alone computers to LANs, WANs and the Web); the capacity to provide complex problems and complex links; functionality (access to sophisticated peripherals); and user friendliness. In the lowest rated quadrant falls computer-aided learning programs based on drill, while approaches which are networked, allowing conferencing between participants, provide access to rich resources, and include challenging tasks that are at the other end of the scale.

The framework of Jones *et al.* (1994) shown in Table 10.1 is based on a conception of engaged learning as meaningful to the learner, collaborative, challenging, multi-disciplinary and oriented around authentic tasks involving important real-world issues. The student is self-regulated and responsible, having optional routes and strategies. It would be inappropriate to evaluate innovations based on these principles by employing a test of traditional teaching designed on transfer of information concepts. In so far as evaluation includes assessment of student achievement, assessment working from this understanding of learning should be interwoven with the learning task, assessing the knowledge constructed by students, observing the processes they adopt and the artefacts they produce.

The models produced by Laurillard (1993) and Jones *et al.* (1994) are not the only ways in which frames of reference can be combined. These examples are based on particular theories of learning and understanding of the possibilities offered by delivery technologies. Other models could have been produced by, for example, a set of criteria based on equity of access to education and training combined with a set of criteria based on the potentials of technology to contribute to learning. This would produce a model of the type shown in Table 10.2.

Applying the frames of reference

Teaching and learning utilizing knowledge media can be evaluated against a great range of possible questions. Sit a team of instructional designers down and they

Table 10.2   *Equity/learning approach matrix*

	Interactive learning technologies	Information transmission learning technologies
Readily accessible technology	eg, simulation on floppy disk	eg, video tape
Difficult to access technology	eg, professional flight simulator	eg, database material on a college server

will come up with dozens of possible evaluation questions and criteria for assessing responses to them. A search of the Internet for criteria + evaluation + education + materials will turn up many possibilities. Yet you will need to generate questions that are appropriate to your situation. Which questions you choose to use depends in part on the frame or frames of reference that are appropriate to the evaluator. The frames of reference provide a rationale for selecting questions and criteria for evaluation. Table 10.3 provides examples of questions that could be used to evaluate teaching and learning utilizing knowledge media and some possible criteria for judging whether responses to the questions are satisfactory. The rationale for including each is derived from the concern or focus of the evaluator indicated by the frame of reference.

Interpreting the results of an evaluation

Summative evaluation of a project involves placing a value upon the product of the project based on data collected about the project and against the criteria employed. As we determine the criteria we will use to evaluate we also determine the way in which the data are interpreted and reported.

Where evaluation is undertaken against the objectives of the particular project, then the interpretative task is to determine whether the data collected indicate that the objectives have been met. Likewise, if the evaluation is a comparative one then the task is to determine whether the data collected indicate that the outcomes obtained are as satisfactory or more satisfactory than those that would have been obtained by using alternative approaches. The answers may often be partial rather than definitive.

Where evaluation is informed by a theoretical understanding about learning, such as constructivism, criteria such as scope for the learner to express his or her own understanding would have been adopted. Evaluation instruments that allow determination of whether such opportunity exists would have been employed. The interpretative task is to place the data collected against the theoretical framework. One might report that a particular knowledge media innovation provided the opportunity for learners to express their own understanding or to demonstrate skills and that this complies with one of the requirements for effective

Table 10.3 *Sample questions and criteria for various frames of reference*

Frame of reference: Objectives–based approach to evaluation

Question	Criteria
Are the objectives stated clearly?	The objectives are stated clearly
What new skills, knowledge and/or attitudes will result from the application of the knowledge media?	The skills, knowledge and/or attitudes likely to be produced match learning objectives
Is information appropriate?	Information is error-free, current, with balanced representations of cultural, ethnic and racial groups
How will the skills, knowledge and attitudes gained during this learning be assessed?	Available assessment will test acquisition of the skills, knowledge and/or attitudes aimed for
In what context will the skills, knowledge and attitudes gained from this learning be used?	The media simulates or approximates the context of users
Does the material contain a tool to measure whether objectives have been met?	The media contains a student assessment instrument pertinent to the objectives

Frame of reference: A focus on the conventional expectations of knowledge media

Question	Criteria
What are the hardware, applications, operating system, and other requirements for operating the knowledge media?	Appropriate facilities are available to the learner, designer, teacher and staff responsible for technical delivery
In what instructional setting will this material be used, eg, learner's workplace, a college laboratory, community library, learner's home?	Appropriate facilities are available in the instructional setting. There is sufficient access guidance and support for the user
Does the knowledge media provide flexibility in location, time and pace of learning?	The media provides flexibility in location, time and pace of learning
Are writing and instructions clear?	Writing and instructions are clear. There is correct use of grammar, spelling, and sentence structure
Are exercise instructions easy to follow?	Exercise instructions are easy to follow
Will the material be enjoyable to use?	Learners will probably enjoy using the knowledge media. The media stimulates imagination and curiosity

Table 10.3 *(continued)*

Frame of reference: A focus on the conventional expectations of knowledge media

Question	Criteria
Is the design of materials of high quality?	Supportive feedback is provided There are options for help Screen displays are uncluttered There are captions, labels, or legends for visuals The typeface is easy to read The layout is attractive The overall look is professional Icons and graphics are used appropriately There is a clear index There is a useful glossary Sound and music are relevant to screen displays The digital technology is bug-free
Is navigation efficient?	The knowledge media offers rapid retrieval of information and screen transitions It uses intuitive icons, menus and directional symbols that foster independent use It is controllable in pace, including options for stop/pause/exit It offers controllable sound
Does the knowledge media offer save and record-keeping features?	The educational innovation has options for: printing/downloading text; save option for games or activities in progress; note-taking feature, when appropriate; record-keeping feature to monitor student progress
Is there a teacher's guide for knowledge media materials?	There is a teacher's guide which offers: a description of target audience; summary of the contents of the application; instructional and/or behavioural objectives; suggestions for classroom use, lesson plans, related activities; ancillary materials for student use, such as camera-ready worksheets and activity pages

Table 10.3   *(continued)*

Frame of reference: Teaching/learning process oriented evaluation

Question	Criteria
What prerequisite knowledge or skills are required before utilizing this knowledge media?	Prerequisites are made known. Learners are likely to have the prerequisites
Are the materials educationally appropriate?	The materials are appropriate to the desired learning outcomes and to the learners' skills, understandings and learning interests
Does the material flow logically with key concepts presented first or introduced appropriately?	The learner can identify key concepts within the learning materials

There is a logical progression of topics with options for increasing complexity |
| Does the knowledge media engender appropriate learner behaviours? | The materials focus on learner behaviour rather than information presentation. The educational media offers a variety of activities, which require the learner to engage skills, knowledge and attitudes appropriate to the intended learning outcomes, eg, the educational innovation provides for creative problem solving |
| Who will be using the knowledge media, eg, students directly, students with the intervention of teachers? | The knowledge media used directly by students is easy to use and has built-in flexibility to cater for varying student needs and responses
The knowledge media used in conjunction with teachers is pertinent to the desired learning outcomes and complements other elements of teaching |
| Does the material adequately cover the subject or the elements of the subject it is intended to cover? | The material covers the area intended or students are directed to other appropriate learning resources. Information is of sufficient scope to adequately cover the topic for the intended audience |
| What educational resources would be needed or could be used to supplement these knowledge media materials? | Lectures, tutorials, seminars, tutor assistance, handouts, bibliographies, videos, etc, that complement or supplement the knowledge media can be identified and made available |

learning situations coming from a constructivist approach. If on the other hand a behaviourist theoretical understanding of learning was employed one would use criteria such as: the learning task is divided into clear steps, correct responses are rewarded and incorrect responses punished or negatively reinforced. The task of the interpretation would then be to determine whether the data collected indicated that clear steps and appropriate rewards and punishments were present. If so, the evaluation report would indicate that the educational innovation establishes an appropriate environment for learning. Different theoretical positions, then, lead to placing value upon different attributes.

Evaluation and cause

Evaluation may indicate the success of the approach used in a project compared to alternative approaches. This leaves open the question of causal factors. Beyond the evaluation of innovations you might like to know what factors are associated with successful digital media projects and what factors with failure, and you might like to be able to make pronouncements on the necessary steps to ensure success with knowledge media. To do so, you need more than an evaluation. You would need to be comfortable with a positivist approach; you would need to conduct an investigation within a theoretical framework; and you would need a way of treating multiple variables in complex educational contexts.

Summary

Evaluation is an aspect of courseware development that needs to be conducted from the outset of a media project and undertaken during the course of a project to inform and modify development. It also needs to be conducted at the end of a project to reflect upon the process and outcomes, to determine appropriate applications of the product and any support or supplementary materials or services that may be necessary, and to inform decisions on similar activities in the future.

The design of evaluation instruments needs to be appropriate to the type of data that need to be collected. Criteria that relate to the rationale underlying the evaluation need to be employed. Evaluation is a matter of attributing value and requires a frame of reference for selecting criteria. Examples of such criteria have been provided in this chapter.

Innovations based on the knowledge media often occur in a context of multiple obligations requiring more than one form of evaluation and implying more than one frame of reference. Data will be interpreted against the premise of the evaluation, such as a theoretical position and according to the criteria which have been chosen to guide the collection of data.

Finally, it should be noted that evaluation is generally not designed to determine cause and effect, for instance what conditions make for effective use of knowledge media. That would require a research exercise rather than an evaluative one.

Chapter 11

Managing the transition

In this chapter we draw on the implementation strategies discussed in this section of the book.

- We discuss the phases of the change process.
- We provide a timetable for sequencing the phases of transition.
- We conclude by identifying a range of principles by means of which it is possible to execute the transition to digital media without at the same time escalating costs.

Organizational responsibility

For most organizations, the transition to electronic delivery will represent a significant shift. It will involve major changes in staffing, procedures, infrastructure and most of all to the culture of the organization. For some organizations that approach the task in a more tentative or exploratory fashion the transition may be less momentous. The significance of the changes to the organization will depend on how critical the transition is to the organization's future and perhaps even to its long-term survival. However, the impact of the transition depends not only on outcomes but also on the efficiency of the transition process itself.

Negotiating the transition successfully depends upon senior management accepting a high degree of responsibility for it. Change management on a large scale cannot succeed without their support. This does not imply that the vision of the project and the planning of its implementation need to be a top-down process. On the contrary, there needs to be ownership, vision and enthusiasm at all levels of the organization. It does, however, mean endorsement of change strategies at the top and support for change agents. It means putting in place project managers for the change strategy as a whole and for particular initiatives within it. In a small organization, the top management may take on this project management function. In large organizations or large departments in organizations it is more appropriate for someone to be given operational responsibility for management of the project.

Project management and evaluation

Existing distance education providers will already be very aware of the crucial importance of project management to the successful conduct of distance education programmes. Institutions and organizations that are coming into this field for the first time are likely not to be as alert to the importance of this role. The types of skills needed for managing the electronic delivery of courses are somewhat different from those needed for the management of print-based delivery, and the skills required for management of the transition to electronic delivery of courses are different again.

One of the most important requirements is familiarity with the characteristics of the range of computer and communications technologies that are used in electronic delivery. Particularly important is awareness of the factors that are likely to impact the learners' experience in learning by this mode – factors such as response times, times taken to download Web pages and failure characteristics of networks.

The role of the project manager

If the transition is to be made smoothly, it will be important for one person to be delegated responsibility for overall operational management of the project. Without this provision, important issues are likely to be missed. If one person holds ultimate responsibility for the success of the project, then that person's duties can be defined in terms of successful completion of the project rather than in terms of particular functions.

The person responsible for operational management of the project will require well-developed skills in the areas of:

- team leadership;
- interpersonal communication;
- time management;
- budget preparation;
- project scheduling;
- reporting writing;
- evaluation procedures;
- group presentation skills.

The person responsible should also possess a good understanding of the educational issues at stake as well as a sound technical knowledge of computer and communications systems.

One of the most important roles that this person will play will be to ensure that the technical infrastructure meets the educational requirements of the project.

Phases of the change process

Most descriptions of innovation involving the new learning technologies examine what is involved in terms of the aspects of the innovation rather than aspects of the change process. For example, Mitchell and Bluer (1996) describe a detailed planning model which is broken up into four stages: initial planning; production; delivery and support; and evaluation. However, making the transition to digital modes of delivery may be better described in terms of the phases of the organizational change process. We consider that there are three major phases to this process: initial planning; start-up; and change-over.

An important aspect of the process of making the transition will be to put in place new organizational structures, policies and procedures for operating in the digital mode. The complexity of the processes and the preparation that are needed make it imperative for them to be initiated and undertaken in parallel if they are to be completed over a reasonable time span. We see the major activity areas as being:

- infrastructure re-engineering;
- staff development;
- courseware development or procurement;
- evaluation;
- support systems.

Phase 1: Developing a proposal

It is standard practice for grant-providing authorities to require applicants for research and innovation funding to set out detailed plans of what they propose. How much more important it is for an organization that may be spending many times the amount offered in a typical research or innovation grant to formulate a detailed proposal. The purpose is the same in each case: to produce a document that ensures that the proponents are clear about the goals, methodology, costs and other requirements of the project and to enable those who are accountable for the resources to discharge their responsibility for ensuring that the funds are well used. With regard to the latter it is essential that estimates of costs are realistic if goals are to be attained (see Chapter 4).

In this initial phase of development it is more appropriate to think of this document as a proposal rather than a plan. What is put forward initially will need the approval of the relevant stakeholders before it can form the basis for action. In the course of gaining stakeholder approval, the details of what is proposed are likely to undergo some change.

The major components that should be incorporated into the proposal include:

- a detailed analysis of what is wanted and why, with supporting evidence;
- a breakdown of the tasks involved;
- a month-by-month schedule for implementation;
- an estimate of staffing requirements;
- infrastructure implications;
- a projected budget.

What is wanted and why?

You need to define the purpose or purposes of the transition to digital delivery:

- Is it an attempt to reduce costs?
- Is it to enhance reputation?
- Is it to improve student learning?
- Is it to promote educational offerings?
- Is it to generate additional income through the marketing of software?

The answers to these questions will determine the nature of the changes that are needed and the best strategy to follow in making those changes. Specifying purposes makes explicit the benefits expected to arise from the project. This can help not only in drafting goals but in stimulating a review of the expectations of adopting digital delivery.

An opportunities analysis

As indicated in Chapter 10, an early step is to undertake an opportunity or market analysis to determine:

- the nature of market opportunities;
- the size of the market;
- the needs of learners.

If it is proposed to make the transition with an existing cohort of students then it will be necessary to establish that the students have the requisite equipment or are willing to acquire it, and whether they are comfortable with the idea of changing their method of delivery.

It is not uncommon for institutions to overestimate the preparedness of students to change their mode of study. If this is found to be the case then it may be better to initiate the transition with a new cohort of students who arrive with the expectation of studying with digital media. Many institutions have started out by launching new full-fee courses on-line.

A task list and schedule

Detailed planning requires a task list and schedule encompassing the range of actions required to effect the transition. A broad schema is provided in Figure 11.1. A more detailed month-by-month schedule, including specification of who is responsible for the actions, will also be needed. A detailed schedule might be drafted at the beginning of each phase.

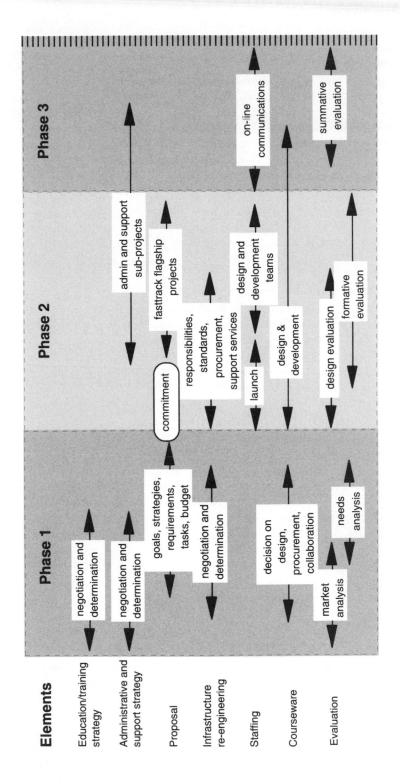

Figure 11.1 *Schedule for managing the transition*

A specification of staff requirements

This concerns the profile and quantity of staff required for the project. If the staffing plan is adopted it may mean some staff redundancies, some staff re-skilling and some recruitment. It is unlikely that the full staffing requirements can be anticipated in advance. However, staffing requirements are the most critical element of the proposal from the point of view of expenditure, often accounting for 70 to 80 per cent of costs, and some indicative estimate is required.

Infrastructure implications

Infrastructure requirements depend upon the education and training strategies proposed and the administrative and support arrangements envisaged, as well as the size of the exercise. At the proposal stage an indication of the infrastructure implications of the proposal, including a costing, is critical to decision making. Next to staffing, technological infrastructure may be the largest cost item.

A projected budget

The project plan will need to include an estimate of the likely costs and returns of the change programme. Costs need to be assessed realistically. They also need to be viewed as one side of the investment equation. The aim is not to minimize costs, but to strike a balance between costs and returns appropriate to the organization's objectives (see Chapters 4 and 5). Under-funded projects can generate worthless outcomes.

Gaining organizational commitment to change

A proposal, when endorsed, earns the organization's commitment to the project. The plan, however, needs to be seen as an evolving document that will be revised in the light of events as the project proceeds. The general thrust of the plan may stay in place but information and communication technologies are continually changing, with the possibility that infrastructure, delivery equipment and software requirements may change. This may have consequences for organizational arrangements and for resource requirements, including staffing.

Depending on the scale and complexity of adopting digital delivery of programmes, detailed planning may be undertaken at the level of minor projects contributing to the overall plan.

Phase 2: Start-up

Re-engineering infrastructure

The extent of technological infrastructure requirements depends upon educational strategies, administrative and support demands and the quality and extent of the existing infrastructure.

It is essential that the systems that are chosen are appropriate for the purposes for which they are required. It is therefore important that the education and training strategies and the administrative and support requirements have been fully worked out before a review of infrastructure requirements commences. These may need to include new arrangements for infrastructure responsibility, in particular arrangements for the allocation of responsibilities between central and local services. Policies for technical standards and for software and hardware compatibility may also need to be revised. An audit of the computers, communications and software already available against the new requirements will determine the extent of re-engineering required.

While the educational and administrative requirements should drive infrastructure re-engineering, technical and supply considerations and costs need to be taken into account. There may need to be some negotiation in the process of determining infrastructure capabilities to ensure that the educational and administrative strategies intended are technically and economically feasible. There may be technical reasons, such as software and hardware compatibility, and supply reasons, such as service agreements, which suggest the acquisition of particular brands of hardware or software. Those responsible for technological infrastructure may also wish to build in a capacity beyond that immediately required in order to meet anticipated requirements. There is a balance in this process between obtaining an infrastructure result which meets present and future requirements and having the infrastructure limit or prescribe the functions available and thus drive educational and administrative strategies.

Acquisition of major items of hardware such as servers and the installation of new communications facilities will almost certainly entail some delay. It is therefore important that decisions on these items be made as early as possible in order to allow sufficient lead-time for installation and commissioning of new systems and the rectification of any faults that are found.

Staff development

The types of activities considered under this heading are the staff development programmes that are specifically planned. Development of the skills of staff will, of course, result from participation in the process, especially in cases where staff are working in teams. However, the management of these opportunities is more subtle.

It is important to get the timing of staff development programmes right. They need to be scheduled for when they will be most effective. Premature development of skills and knowledge can be ineffective because the newly-acquired skills cannot be consolidated and extended. On the other hand, delays in the provision of staff development can cause frustration and also erode the commitment of staff to the proposed developments. A 'just-in-time' approach is required. However, this may have logistical implications for a large organization.

There are three stages at which the conduct of formal staff development activities are likely to prove particularly beneficial. The first stage needs to occur when the programme is being launched. Gaining the commitment of staff is important for the success of organizational change of this magnitude and providing an occasion which both symbolizes the beginning of a new era for the organization and informs staff what is planned and what to expect is part of that process.

An appropriate form for a launch event to take might be a forum or series of fora at which visiting speakers who have already been involved in such a process outline their own experiences and demonstrate products on which they have worked.

The second stage is when the development of new courseware is being initiated. During this phase of the transition, teaching staff will require training in the procedures and processes that will be followed in the design and development stages of preparing courseware. If it has been determined that a team approach to development will be followed, then it will be important that all the members of each development team understand the contributions that they are expected to make and the contributions that other members of the team will be making. Development of staff skills can be undertaken as part of the collaborative work of the team. The choice of team leaders will be important in ensuring that team members are supported.

The third stage during which staff development will be important will be when new course delivery modes are being implemented, particularly during the initial trials. For many teaching staff the use of computer-mediated communication to support online tutorials will be a new experience. The accent in training will need to be on the pedagogical aspects of using this form of interaction with students. However, staff can be familiarized with communication elements – such as e-mail, document transfer, bulletin boards and discussion sites – by using these systems for communication among staff.

Courseware development or acquisition

Decisions need to be made about the extent to which digital resources will be developed in-house or involve bringing-in expertise, contracting-out assignments or procuring existing materials. Decisions in this area need to be made following market and needs analyses and concurrently with the early stages of a staff development programme. Opportunities to procure and adapt available materials need to be reviewed from time to time as needs become clearer some way into a project and as new materials come on the market.

In so far as it is decided to design and develop materials in-house or through collaboration, decisions need to be made about the extent to which this will be achieved through specialization of functions and the extent to which it will be in the hands of teachers and trainers. Staff development will need to be tailored accordingly.

Implementation of new support systems

A separate implementation programme will need to be set out for each of the new support systems that is being implemented. The time frame for implementation will differ according to the system. Implementation of each support system will include infrastructure and staff development components. The task of managing the introduction of each support system may be seen as a complete sub-project, with all the attributes of the larger project.

Evaluation

Market and needs analyses will have been undertaken in developing a proposal, as indicated above. Design evaluation and formative evaluation are required during courseware design and development to avoid the need to redesign media products and to ensure their applicability to the anticipated clientele.

Courseware available on the market also needs to be evaluated at an early stage for its suitability to the project's purposes (see Chapter 10).

Phase 3: Change-over

The change-over phase is likely to extend over a long period, perhaps years. It will be characterized by successive mainstreaming of electronic delivery functions and involvement of an increasing proportion of teaching staff. The change-over process will amount to a repetition of the processes adopted in the start-up phase, modified in the light of information provided by the evaluation of these processes.

It would be reasonable to expect the processes in this phase to proceed more smoothly, more rapidly and with greater confidence on the part of staff.

Strategies for managing costs

One of the important management functions in making the transition to the knowledge media is managing costs. If you are aware that there is a risk of the costs of electronic delivery rising above those of print-based or face-to-face delivery, then it is important to have strategies for containing costs which don't adversely affect the quality of teaching or return on investment. The following strategies are some that are suggested by what we already know about the cost-effectiveness of using the various digital media in the delivery of education and training programmes.

Deliver courses in parallel forms

The same design and development costs apply to print and online delivery. Yet the cost of translating textual materials into HTML is small, especially when using current generation Web authoring tools. This allows you to obtain maximum economies of scale while still enabling you to start making the transition to on-line delivery. Delivery via alternative media enables you to tap both traditional distance education and online markets while the demand for online delivery grows. The major disadvantage of this approach is that it limits the extent to which you can take advantage of the unique possibilities of the World Wide Web.

Be selective in the development of interactive multimedia courseware

Producing interactive multimedia courseware is much more costly than producing textual materials. The use of interactive multimedia should be targeted at applications for which video, animation or interactive elements offer specific advantages. Interactive multimedia projects should be carefully planned and their cost justified in terms of the contribution they will make to improving the quality of student learning or decreasing the time taken to reach specified outcomes. Look for opportunities to procure suitable interactive multimedia, together with rights to modify or supplement it if necessary.

Look for opportunities for collaboration in expensive courseware development projects

The high costs of development of interactive multimedia courseware can be partly accommodated by entering into collaborative ventures with other providers that have similar needs and interests.

Give responsibility for multimedia programming and Web page design to production staff

The cost of training teaching staff in multimedia programming and Web page design can never be recouped from the small number of projects on which such staff will be able to use these skills. Furthermore, without a significant investment in ongoing training, the skills will soon become out of date. Over the medium and longer term, the cost of employing or hiring multimedia programmers and Web page designers will be amply repaid as a result of shorter lead-in and production times and higher production values.

Carefully target staff development programmes

Staff development is important in giving staff the skills they need to work efficiently and effectively in the new teaching and learning environment. However, giving staff skills they do not require and will not use is both wasteful of resources and confusing for the staff involved. Staff development initiatives need to be keyed to the organization's programme for realignment of its delivery modes.

Seek multiple uses for expensively produced multimedia courseware

Economies of scale apply just as much to the development of small segments of instruction as they do to developing whole subjects. Interactive multimedia projects with high fixed costs require more students to bring down the cost per student to that of media forms with lower fixed costs. One way of accommodating the higher costs of interactive multimedia products is therefore to find multiple uses for them. The smaller the size of a courseware module, the more likely it is that it can find a use somewhere else in a teaching programme.

Provide a clear structure for computer conferencing sessions

Experience with the use of computer conferencing for promoting interaction among students shows that effective student participation depends on providing a clear structure, with specific tasks, and tutors being actively involved in promoting interaction among participants. Once group members feel that they know each other and the tutor they will be much more ready to take the lead in promoting discussion. This suggests initial face-to-face contact if practicable. Computer conferencing is most economical where a group is involved. It can be oriented to group work.

Encourage the establishment of peer support groups

If the staffing costs of tutoring online are high, there is scope for achieving significant savings by enabling students to support each other. One of the benefits of computer-mediated communication is that it allows students to communicate with each other in groups. Students can form study groups in a virtual study centre. Teachers can monitor the operation of study groups and offer support where needed, rather than being the centre of communication.

However, be careful not to take students' capacity to use this new medium too much for granted. If they are to use the medium effectively they will need to be given some initial training in its use.

The time involved in these activities will not be negligible. It needs to be included in the overall budget.

Summary

The transition process may be conceived of as taking place in three phases:

- planning;
- start-up;
- change-over.

The planning stage is concerned with 'thinking through' the change process, developing a change programme and gaining the commitment of all parts of the organization to the proposed programme.

The start-up phase is focused on implementing and testing new systems, processes and procedures and piloting new methods of development and delivery.

The change-over phase is concerned with extending the tested systems, processes and procedures across the whole organization. This phase may last several years.

The purpose of organizational change is generally to increase efficiency and thereby save costs. However, there is a cost attached to the change process itself. Whether a process does in the end yield the expected savings can only be gauged much later. Managing costs in the context of change therefore involves the considered application of well-established cost-saving principles.

Section III: QUALITY ASSURANCE

Chapter 12

A quality assurance framework for achieving best practice in new learning technologies

In this chapter we define the concept of 'best practice' in relation to teaching and learning and describe the benefits of implementing a quality assurance strategy for digital delivery.

We provide a comprehensive 'best practice' framework that can be used by managers as a tool for the implementation and quality assurance of new learning technologies.

To help managers implement a quality procedure we provide a case study of the use of the framework in practice.

The demand for quality

Changes in the economic climate and technology are providing both opportunities and challenges for education and training organizations to redefine their educational paradigms.

High-quality, interactive learning materials exemplify potentially new and exciting ways of approaching the provision of education and training and address-

ing the increasing demands of learners for access. There is now widespread
agreement that these new technologies have the potential to:

- serve a greater and more diverse student body;
- make significant improvements in the quality of student learning while at
  the same time containing the expensive infrastructure costs and the labour-
  intensive lecture of the campus–bound classroom.

The demand for 'quality' in education and training has never been greater.
Students, governments, funding bodies and the community expect an education
system that delivers quality products, services and graduates and makes the best
use of their money. At the same time, education and training providers are also
operating in a new, competitive market where student demands cannot be taken
for granted. Rather, students and employees will be attracted to education and
training organizations that offer products and services that come closest to meeting
their needs as they perceive them. In this competitive environment, education
and training organizations must therefore:

- be flexible and responsive;
- develop quality systems and management processes;
- meet the needs and expectation of their customers and clients.

With the new technologies driving the change from traditional delivery methodologies to a more open and client-centred approach, the effective use of new
learning technologies is often seen by writers in the field as a key factor in meeting
the triple challenge faced by education and training organizations:

- providing a high-quality education;
- to all students who need and can benefit from it.;
- in the most cost–effective way.

Many education and training organizations have already adapted their delivery
strategies to take advantage of new developments in the information and communications fields and are making considerable investment in the development
of their technological infrastructure. Education and training organizations must
therefore assure themselves that the perceived benefits, especially in tight fiscal
environments, justify the costs. In order to reap the benefits for which they are
hoping, and to ensure that the quality of programmes is not compromised,
management needs to develop comprehensive quality assurance processes to
evaluate the impact of these new learning technologies.

There is a growing recognition among education and training providers that
an increased focus on concepts and strategies borrowed from the corporate sector
and directed at achieving 'world best practice' are critical in addressing this
problematic relationship between quality and competitiveness in education and
training organizations.

It is in this context that we have developed a quality assurance framework
that provides the basis for improving the quality of provision of new learning
technologies in education and training.

The quality agenda in education and training

Quality as a discipline has its roots in the aftermath of World War II, when a devastated Japan was helped by US consultants in the restructuring of its manufacturing industries. Gradually, other industries across the world, including non-manufacturing industries and even service industries like education, recognized the necessity of applying 'quality principles' to the daily business of work. Applying these 'quality principles' in organizations has generally contributed to improved capability, be it in terms of productivity, more satisfied customers, or – in education and training – the provision of better courses.

While it is not possible to define quality in education in the same way that manufacturing organizations might define the quality of their products, it is possible to identify practices that are effective in producing quality learning outcomes.

The concept of best practice

Best practice is a comprehensive, integrated and cooperative approach to the continuous improvement of all facets of an organization's operations. It is the way leading-edge organizations manage their operations to deliver world-class standards of performance. In general, the features of best practice companies are those that simultaneously improve the quality, cost and delivery of their products or services, use technology to advantage and maintain close links with their customers and stakeholders.

An Australian study of international best practice (Department of Industrial Relations and Australian Manufacturing Council, 1992) identified the following as components of best practice:

- strong leadership from top management in developing a vision and implementing a strategy for world-class performance;
- extensive consultation and communication with employees to develop a shared understanding and commitment to corporate goals and strategies;
- a focus on simultaneous improvement in cost, quality and delivery;
- better utilization of existing technology and the adoption of the most appropriate advanced technology;
- implementation of education and training programmes to enhance and broaden the skills of employees;
- commitment from employees through increasing the breadth of their decision making and involvement in traditional management responsibilities;
- closer links with suppliers and customers;
- a culture in which everybody is encouraged to make ongoing improvements in the way they work;
- integrated approaches and less hierarchical structures for greater flexibility;
- human resource policies that promote continuous learning, teamwork, participation and flexibility.

A definition of best practice in education

In Australia, the Committee for Quality Assurance in Higher Education (CQAHE) was established by the Keating government to review and rank Australian universities against a set of teaching and learning criteria. These included course design, delivery and assessment and staff recruitment processes. The CQAHE defined quality assurance in the area of teaching and learning as:

> the totality of the arrangements by which an organization discharges its responsibility for the quality of the teaching it offers, satisfying itself that the mechanisms for quality control are effective and promote improvement.

In its report on the quality review of teaching and learning, the CQAHE (1995: 3–8) identified the following characteristics of good teaching and learning:

- an institution-wide approach to planning and management;
- integrated university-wide processes for evaluating, monitoring and review;
- use of national and international benchmarking;
- course approval procedures;
- use of external stakeholders in course design and review;
- matching of delivery style to learning needs of particular groups of students;
- monitoring of examination standards and mark scaling;
- rigour of staff appointment procedures;
- weight given to teaching skills in promotion;
- staff appraisal systems;
- opportunities and programmes for the improvement of teaching skills;
- innovation in the area of teaching and learning;
- alignment of student services to the institutional mission including the targeting of support;
- access to and availability of effective student services, especially library and information technology;
- provision for effective student participation on university committees;
- practical implementation of student grievance procedures;
- feedback on changes resulting from student surveys.

While the focus of the two investigations is different, there is a remarkable degree of similarity between the two findings. Globally too, there is recognition of the convergence of a set of universal 'best practice' principles and quality concepts that have emerged from the experience of 'best practice' organizations.

In Australia, like the United States, Europe and Japan, this convergence has led to the development of very similar and internationally recognized models of best practice. For example:

- The Baldrige Award in the United States
- The European Quality Award
- The Deming Prize in Japan
- The Business Excellence Framework in Australia.

These models have been adopted as a way of driving improvements in performance in organizations and to move enterprises towards world best practice.

For example, the Malcolm Baldrige National Quality Award was established in 1987 as an annual US National Quality Award. The award is named after Malcolm Baldrige, who served as Secretary of Commerce from 1981. His managerial excellence contributed to long-term improvements in efficiency and effectiveness in the US government.

The purpose of the award is to promote quality awareness and an understanding of the requirements for performance excellence. Applicants must address seven categories, which describe an agreed set of standards that reflect current understanding of best practice and characteristics of quality organizations. The seven categories are:

- leadership;
- strategic planning;
- customer and market focus;
- information and analysis;
- human resource focus;
- process management;
- business results.

These seven categories indicate the importance of:

- a commitment to change throughout the organization driven by the full and public support of the leadership of the organization;
- a strategic plan, developed in consultation with the workforce, which encompasses all aspects of an organization's operations and which sets out short, medium and long term goals;
- flatter organizational structures supported by the devolution of responsibility, the empowerment of the workers and improved communication. This often involves team-based work structures;
- a commitment to continuous improvement and learning, with a highly-skilled and flexible workforce and a recognition of the value of all people in the organization;
- focusing on data and evidence to reach decisions and the use of performance measurement systems and benchmarking;
- quality as defined by the customer.

These 'best practice' categories or criteria are similar in each of the quality awards around the world. The criteria can therefore be considered to be the critical elements that define a 'best practice' organization.

The Baldrige model can be accessed on the World Wide Web on <http://www.quality.nist.gov/docs/98_crit/98crit.htm>

The United States is the most competitive nation in the world. Quality is a key to retaining that title. The Malcolm Baldrige National Quality Award is helping US companies satisfy customers and improve overall company performance and capabilities.

William J Clinton

Many organizations now recognize the potential that exists for improving their competitiveness by assessing themselves against these models of business excellence. As a consequence the models are increasingly being used in both private and public sector enterprises to drive quality improvement initiatives.

When combined with a self-assessment approach, these models identify opportunities for improvement and provide measures of the organization's quality journey.

Applying models of best practice to education and training

Many enterprises have been convinced that applying quality and 'best practice' principles contributes to productivity; that it is possible to do more with less and to do it better while at the same time containing costs. Education and training providers confront the same issues as other organizations in other industries. They must satisfy their students (customers), manage change, manage people within a changing environment, allocate resources and plan for long-term viability. Funding cuts, pressures to increase provision and the need to develop greater accountability have made it imperative that education and training organizations follow a 'best practice' approach.

Quality is not a new concept in education. However, it is only relatively recently that educational institutions began considering the formal application of quality principles to their practices.

It is taken for granted that education and training providers should be accountable for the quality of their activities. The pace of technological change and the necessity of public accountability and competitive pressures have increased to the point where a fundamental requirement for education and training organizations is a capacity to manage change and improvement. Organizations need to assure their customers that the services they offer are carried out as intended.

In 1995, the National Institute of Standards and Technology in the United States piloted programmes to adapt the Malcolm Baldrige best practice model to educational organizations. They concluded that the model was as applicable to educational organizations as it was to the manufacturing sector.

In 1996, the Australian National Training Authority conducted a similar exercise. They too concluded that the model was a suitable and practical tool for evaluating and describing key improvement strategies for educational organizations.

The quality concepts and principles embodied in these international 'best practice' models have provided the basis for a quality assurance framework for the provision of online learning and new learning technologies.

A quality assurance framework for best practice in new learning technologies

The intention of the framework is to provide a systematic tool that enables managers to assess the implementation of new learning technologies against a model that defines 'best practice'. The framework provides an approach to assessing the quality provision of new learning technologies in education and training organizations.

The primary purpose of the framework is to provide a set of principles and best practice indicators which address the essential areas in the quality provision of online learning and new learning technologies and against which managers can assess the extent to which they have achieved 'best practice'.

Both technology and innovative teaching and learning practices are developing so rapidly that any description of 'best practice' is likely to be out of date by the time it is published, and this framework is no exception. We therefore take the view that the notion of best practice is not one that can be packaged and defined for the long term.

Components of the framework

The framework involves principles, indicators and a checklist, as shown in Figure 12.1. There are 10 essential principles for implementing or assessing best practice for online learning. For each principle there is a set of indicators that identify when best practice has been achieved. Strategies to achieve best practice can then be developed by course teams using checklists that specify documentary evidence of best practice for the various indicators.

The 10 principles related to the development of 'best practice' for the provision of quality new learning technologies are:

1. informed planning and management of resources;
2. sustained committed leadership;
3. improving access for all clients, incorporating equity and promoting cultural diversity;
4. understanding the requirements of the learner and reflecting stakeholder requirements;
5. the design, development and implementation of programmes for effective and active learning;
6. creating confident and committed staff with new competencies;
7. managing and maintaining the technical infrastructure;
8. evaluating for continuous improvement;
9. providing effective and efficient administrative systems and services;
10. supporting the needs of learners.

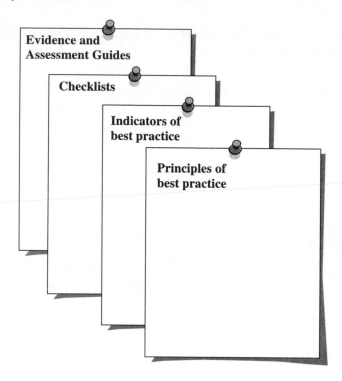

The framework is a nested framework and identifies 10 essential principles to consider when implementing good practice.

Each principle lists a range of indicators which identify when good practice has been achieved. Strategies to achieve good practice are developed by each team. Checklists and assessment guides can be developed by course teams as evidence that they have achieved good practice.

Figure 12.1   *Structure of the framework*

These principles, while being broad enough to be applicable to any organization, are sufficiently explicit to enable education and training organizations to develop quality processes for the delivery of online learning and new learning technology programmes.

Indicators of best practice

Each principle is linked with statements which indicate recognized and acknowledged best practice. The best practice indicators have been gathered from research, case studies and successful practitioners in the field. The indicators define areas of best practice thereby providing a basis for comparison. While these best practice statements do not specify clearly defined strategies for the achievement of best practice, they do provide managers with best practice targets against which they can identify their own strategies as they journey towards best practice.

A best practice framework for the delivery of online learning and new learning technology programmes

Principle 1. Best practice for online learning and new learning technologies involves informed planning and management of resources

Corporate policies and mission statements adopted by the organization must include reference to new learning technologies as a component of its teaching and learning strategies.

The organization ensures that suitably trained people, facilities and infrastructure are adequate and available for the provision of online learning.

Indicators of best practice

- There is evidence that online learning and new learning technology programmes are being integrated across all planning levels within the institution, including financial, human resource and support service planning.
- Corporate policies and mission statements (or equivalent) identify the broad-based educational objective of new learning technology programmes.
- Organizational structures are flexible and responsive and assist the implementation of new learning technologies across all departments and faculties.
- The institution employs communication processes which lead to a clear sense of purpose and direction in the development and delivery of new learning technologies.
- A management plan for the provision and implementation of new learning technologies has been developed, with a time schedule including identification of critical events.
- Organizational strategies include the development of mainstream new learning technology programmes as well as the piloting of innovations.
- Performance indicators for new learning technology programmes have been identified.
- Efficient and equitable resource allocation models are developed and adopted.
- Collaborative arrangements with other educational institutions and with the corporate sector are in place to ensure effective access to and use of resources.
- A realistic costing of all aspects of development, trial and (as far as is measurable) implementation of new learning technology activities has been made.
- Resources (financial, material, human) are available to support all aspects of development, trial and implementation of new learning technologies.

- The institution has a process in place to ensure that the equipment and materials are sufficient for the provision of new learning technologies for students with special needs or disabilities.
- The organization has defined the constituencies it intends to serve as well as the parameters under which new learning technologies programmes can be offered and resources allocated.
- A human resources development plan has been formed based on an analysis of the tasks required for development, delivery and support of new learning technologies.

Principle 2. Best practice for online learning and new learning technologies involves sustained, committed leadership

Leadership style and behaviour is critical in ensuring that the organization's goals for new learning technologies are achieved.

Institutional support for the development and use of new learning technologies is a critical prerequisite for its widespread adoption and integration into mainstream programmes.

Indicators of best practice

- Appropriate performance indicators have been developed for the monitoring and evaluation of new learning technologies.
- Leadership behaviour demonstrates commitment to the provision and maintenance of new learning technologies and ongoing improvement processes.
- Policies and practices are developed to support the provision of new learning technologies.
- There is a commitment to providing the level of complex technical and online support required to run efficient, reliable and 'user friendly' systems.
- Communication systems are open and multi-directional.
- A realistic costing of all aspects of new learning technologies developments, pilots and implementation phases has been made.
- The impact of new learning technologies on existing physical facilities has been assessed.
- Leadership behaviour demonstrates commitment to an organization-wide approach to improving teaching and learning through the use of new learning technologies.
- The impact and outcomes of new learning technologies for existing managerial, administrative and physical facilities has been assessed.

Principle 3. Best practice for online learning and new learning technologies involves improving access for all clients, incorporates equity and promotes cultural diversity

The provision of new learning technologies improves the access, participation and success rates of under-represented groups.

Learning opportunities ensure that learners are not limited in their engagement due to physical location, disability, race, ethnicity, level of technological skills or level of access to physical resources, and that their level of language and literacy skills is taken into account. New learning technology programmes are accessible to all students irrespective of income and location. The organization actively seeks diversity.

Indicators of best practice

- Indicators to establish access, participation and success rates for equity groups are collected, reviewed and acted upon.
- Barriers that prevent current and potential students accessing new learning technology products and services are identified and strategies to improve access and participation are implemented.
- The organization conducts research and monitors the emergence of new equity groups (eg, those lacking in information competence).
- The institution fosters an affirmative environment in which diversity is embraced and every person is treated with respect.
- New learning technology performance indicators have been established for each equity group.
- Courseware development for new learning technologies accommodates the background, skills and interests of equity groups.
- Delivery media are selected on the basis of 'best fit' between learner effectiveness, accessibility and cost.
- Programmes do not impose prohibitive attendance requirements, or unnecessarily control the pace of learning, or restrict entry and exit options.
- Technologies used enable improved access for disadvantaged groups and work-based learners.

Principle 4. Best practice for online learning and new learning technologies involves understanding the requirements of the learner and reflects stakeholder requirements

The main focus of developments in new learning technologies is the needs of learners, clients and stakeholders. The organization has a student-centred approach to new learning technologies that is soundly based in an understanding of learners' characteristics and needs. Stakeholder requirements are reflected in the provision of new learning technologies.

Indicators of best practice

- The planning stages of new learning technology provision take into account the intended learners' objectives, cognitive level, learning styles and access requirements, and the demands of the curriculum.
- New learning technology policies and practices make clear the organization's obligations to its learners and the learners' obligations to the institution.
- An appropriate range of resources is available to accommodate student learning.
- A process for assessing customer requirements and satisfaction is developed and implemented.
- External and internal clients and stakeholders have been identified (eg, government agencies, community groups) and their needs and expectations are reflected in new learning technology policy and processes.

Principle 5. Best practice for online learning and new learning technologies involves the design, development and implementation of programmes for effective and active learning

Course design, development and implementation processes are sufficiently rigorous to ensure that courses meet the requirements of learners, industry and the professions and are effective in achieving learning outcomes.

Indicators of best practice

Course design

- The design of new learning technology programmes is informed by research on learning.
- The responsibility for design, approval, implementation and revision of new learning technology courses is vested in designated bodies with clearly established channels of communication, control and review.
- Course design, development and implementation processes are sufficiently flexible to adapt to the prior experiences of learners, their learning needs and situations.
- Course design is structured and incorporates interactive instruction techniques mediated by human intervention and a supportive learning environment.
- Programme design encourages a realistic progression towards self-direction and recognizes varied starting points in levels of confidence and motivation.

- Courseware is designed to suit the characteristics of learners, provide a clear learning pathway, reinforce important concepts and promote active learning.
- Programme and course objectives clearly specify the subject matter to be covered, the intellectual skills to be acquired and the learning methods used.
- Course assessment is related to intended learning outcomes and to students' learning needs and situations.
- Learning-to-learn strategies are incorporated into all course units.
- Course design processes reflect desired graduate attributes.

Course development

- Policies and procedures for additions and deletions of programmes and courses are carefully planned and implemented and are consistent with the resources of the organization, staff capabilities and the needs of stakeholders.
- Programme, design, development and accreditation processes are systematically reviewed and opportunities for improvement identified to ensure the continued relevance of programmes.

Assessment

- Criteria for evaluating student performance are clearly established, stated in course guidelines and are generally understood by students and staff.
- Assessment practices are fair, valid and reliable and allow for a variety of circumstances.
- Assessment practices reward competence in the process of learning as well as knowledge of content.

Principle 6. Best practice for online learning and new learning technologies involves creating confident and committed staff with new competencies

The organization recruits, manages and provides development opportunities for its staff to ensure that they have the skills to meet client-focused new learning technology programmes.

Indicators of best practice

- Subject expertise and technical and instructional design expertise are available to develop and support quality new learning technology programmes.
- Professional development for the provision of new learning technologies, for all categories of staff, are identified and suitable arrangements made.
- Best practice in new learning technologies is effectively disseminated to staff for formal or informal education and training.

- Staff development provision meets organizational and individual development needs for the effective provision of new learning technologies.
- Appropriate cross-functional project teams address specific requirements of new learning technology projects.
- Staff development processes for new learning technology activities are equitable, well-resourced and systematically implemented.
- Changes to staff roles and work practices as a result of changes to teaching and learning are recognized, and there is a well-resourced consultative process undertaken to address industrial relations issues.
- Procedures and incentives are in place to encourage staff to make appropriate and innovative use of electronic information resources to improve the academic programme, publish scholarly information, and to encourage equitable student use.

Principle 7. Best practice involves managing and maintaining the technical infrastructure to support online learning and new learning technologies

Decisions about the choice of technology are driven by consideration of learners' needs, the ability of teachers and other staff to provide support for learners, and the curriculum content of the programme. Resource materials are of sound quality, suitable for the purpose, and well-matched with available technologies and staff capabilities.

Indicators of best practice

- Information technology strategies support the implementation of new learning technologies.
- The choice of technology, including the delivery method, reflects learners' needs, the curriculum content of the programme and human resource availability.
- The technology is supported by a technology plan that includes:
  - how the technology is to be used for learning;
  - how people are to be trained to use the technology;
  - how the technology is to be managed and maintained.
- Stand-alone and networked computing systems are used as a tool to support individualized learning and to enhance access to resources.
- The relevance of different technologies to different learning approaches is understood.
- A decision has been made about the support mechanisms that should be associated with technology and resource materials and the way in which these components interrelate.

- There is an institution-wide coordination of the process for evaluating and acquiring emerging technologies.
- Information technology standards are in place and members of the institution are aware of these so that they can make an informed choice when purchasing new technology.
- Software, hardware and network resources are appropriate in quantity and quality to meet academic programme needs.
- Decisions have been made about the extent to which equipment will be provided to learners (eg, on loan, or by access in a library).
- Funding, staff time and skills are available to operate the technology and provide technical support for teachers and learners.
- Decisions have been made whether to buy in or adapt existing learning materials or to develop new materials.
- The copyright and intellectual property implications of buying, licensing or developing materials have been explored, and processes are in place conforming with policy.

Principle 8. Best practice for online learning and new learning technologies involves evaluating for continuous improvement

The organization evaluates and continuously improves its provision of new learning technologies. New learning technology initiatives are continuously informed by the evaluation of learning outcomes, equity considerations, cost-effectiveness and stakeholder satisfaction.

Indicators of best practice

- The organization continuously monitors and measures the effectiveness and efficiency of new learning technology programmes as part of its continuous improvement process.
- Courses are systematically reviewed to assess their effectiveness.
- Data and information, rather than hunches, are the basis for all decision making.
- Qualitative and quantitative data regarding student outcomes are used to measure the effectiveness and efficiency of key new learning technology processes.
- Performance indicators have been identified, eg, increased participation, faster student throughput, higher student retention, higher enrolments/re-enrolments, improved graduate attributes, improved access for workers and disadvantaged groups.
- The organization regularly benchmarks its new learning technology processes and outcomes against other organizations.
- New learning technology outcomes are regularly benchmarked against learning outcomes in mainstream courses to ensure consistency.

- The organization provides for formal investigations and specific action to deal with student complaints.

Principle 9. Best practice for online learning and new learning technologies involves the provision of effective and efficient administrative services

The organization provides administrative services that support and complement the provision of new learning technologies.

Indicators of best practice

- The impact and outcomes of new learning technologies on existing managerial, administrative and other procedures are taken into account.
- Management information systems are flexible and take into account all aspects of new learning technology activities, including student enrolment, production scheduling, delivery processes, planning and costing mechanisms, and meet the demands of stakeholders in terms of time frames, reliability and accessibility.
- Administrative processes facilitate learner progress while allowing maximum flexibility in programme choice.
- Administrative information resources are provided electronically so as to increase the effectiveness and efficiency of the institution.
- There is ready electronic access to information resources such as bulletin boards, with sufficient capacity to supply high-volume data where appropriate.

Principle 10. Best practice for online learning and new learning technologies supports the needs of learners

The needs for student learning and technical and personal support for new learning technology programmes are identified, provided for and regularly reviewed. Decisions on the comprehensiveness of services depend on the purposes of the institution and the diversity of its student body.

Indicators of best practice

- Constraints and opportunities for learner support have been analysed and support structures, including interaction with teachers, trainers or facilitators, are in place.
- A decision has been made about the extent to which equipment will be provided to learners (eg, on loan, or by access in a library), and the extent to which equipment must be provided for staff use.

- The organization systematically studies the characteristics of its student cohort and identifies the support needs of the student population.
- The institution has an organized system for admission, assessment, orientation, support and student follow-up compatible with the circumstances of students.
- Student publications describe relevant new learning technology policies and procedures.
- Institute staff working in new learning technology programmes coordinate their efforts and work in collaboration with library and other student learning support staff.
- The total costs of new learning technology programmes are made explicit to students.
- Support services are provided to enable all students to participate effectively in courses and to enhance their success in achieving their educational outcomes.
- Precise, accurate and current information is provided in information to students concerning:
  - (a) educational purposes;
  - (b) degrees, curricular offerings;
  - (c) student fees and other financial obligations, student financial aid, and fee refund policies;
  - (d) requirements for admission and for achievement of degrees;
  - (e) assessment processes.
- Policies on students' rights and responsibilities, including the rights of due process and redress of grievances and rules defining inappropriate student conduct, are clearly stated, well-publicized and readily available and they are implemented in a fair and consistent manner.
- The institution makes provision for the security of student records of admission and progress. Student records, including transcripts, are private, accurate, complete and permanent. They are protected by fireproof and otherwise safe storage and backed by duplicate files. Data and records maintained in computing systems have adequate security and provision for recovery from disasters.
- Educational programmes address differing skill levels of users, and strategies provide online help and support facilities.
- The organization's telecommunications centres, library, technological infrastructure and computing laboratories are appropriate for the academic programmes and the nature of the institution.

Implementing the framework – a user guide for managers

The framework is intended to foster the development and implementation of quality arrangements tailored to the needs and circumstances of individual education and training organizations.

While it is unlikely that any single prescriptive best practice framework can be applied to all situations, the framework provides a broad platform to underpin the quality arrangements adopted by each organization.

The framework offers a systematic means of reviewing, measuring and improving the delivery of online learning. By using the framework either in team discussions or through a more rigorous self-assessment approach, managers can begin to identify and improve the processes that are critical to implementing and developing quality new learning technology programmes and online operations.

Advantages of using the framework

The framework has the potential to:

- identify and prioritize improvement targets to ensure resources are allocated effectively;
- provide a structured approach to assessing where you want to be;
- integrate improvement activities into normal operations;
- encourage staff to share successful approaches and to embrace continual improvement practices;
- generate opportunities to recognize progress and reward the achievement of results;
- provide an indication of how far and how successfully planned activities have been adopted throughout the organization;
- provide hard data and evidence, rather than individual perceptions or anecdotal data, with which to reach conclusions;
- enhance team spirit and enthusiasm through staff involvement;
- provide a common basis for reporting performance;
- provide a tool to benchmark performance with other organizations.

Best practice statements – finding the answers

We do not believe that anyone outside the organization can come up with the most appropriate way to implement best practice. We expect that organizations will make informed choices about ways to proceed that are most suited to themselves and their learners at a particular time.

Managers may find that there are no easy strategies to best practice solutions in their organization. For example, it can be difficult to find really good solutions to some of the aspects of industrial relations that arise from implementing online learning throughout the organization. In this case we suggest that you use the statements as the basis of discussion in your organization and to help you think through your approach.

There are many helpful resources in the system which can lead you to the solution of any particular problem; many of these are on the World Wide Web.

The framework has been structured for a range of uses. Primarily it is a tool for managers in organizations that are developing or implementing the delivery of online learning and new learning technologies.

1. Using the framework as a planning tool

Managers and practitioners who are considering using new learning technologies to deliver or support learning can use the framework as a planning tool.

Individuals or teams can use the framework to guide them in making good planning decisions. For example, prior to implementing a new learning technology programme, managers should develop comprehensive implementation plans. The indicators will help in the development of these plans and consideration of those areas critical to its success. The framework may also indicate priority areas for the allocation of resources and quality initiatives.

2. Using the framework as a self-assessment tool for continuous improvement

Using the framework as an evaluation or self-assessment tool was initially promoted through the various international models of best practice. Organizations using such models are able to measure systematically their progress and determine whether their products, services and management processes meet the quality criteria of the model. The results of this self-assessment process are then used to identify and prioritize improvement opportunities. This framework can be used in a similar way to evaluate completed projects against the best practice principles and indicators.

3. Using the framework as a basis for professional development activities

The framework can also be used as a foundation for staff development programmes. A staff development programme could be designed to develop an understanding of concepts related to the use of new learning technologies and the identification and solution of real-life problems. Managers might choose to set up one or two project teams which would identify problems or decisions that need to be made, and use the framework both as a source of information and as a guide for discussion of the learning.

Implementing the framework – a case study

The following case study shows how the framework can be implemented at a post-secondary institution.

Step 1. Gaining acceptance and integration into policy

In order for the framework to gain acceptance across the organization, it was presented to several key committees for adoption into policy. An implementation committee was formed, which recommended that the framework be shortened, contextualized and piloted.

Step 2. Steps to contextualizing the framework

In this case, the committee decided to use the framework as a staff development tool.

The implementation committee felt that the framework was too long for practical use by course teams. They identified the most important four or five indicators from the framework and contextualized these to the organization's procedures.

The committee also eliminated those indicators over which course team leaders did not have direct control. For example, in principle 7 the following indicator was eliminated as it applied across the whole organization: 'There is an institution-wide coordination of the process for evaluating and acquiring emerging technologies'.

The committee also felt uncomfortable with the idea of developing 'best practice'; they believed that best practice was really a moving target and preferred the term 'good practice framework'

Step 3. Prioritizing improvement activities

Course teams, using the 'good practice' indicators as a guide, identified and prioritized improvement activities for their online course delivery (see the worked example of the improvement matrix in Figure 12.2).

For example, one course team who had received funding to develop a new online course for 'Accounting 1', failed to convince management of the need for ongoing funding for their online course. They had not gathered enough evidence for the continuing viability of their online trial.

This course team identified one of their improvement activities as being the development and comparison of client satisfaction and enrolment data for both their online and lecture-based courses. Lecturers were convinced that client satisfaction data and improved enrolment figures would indicate that students were much happier with the flexibility offered by the online accounting subject than the lecture-based subject.

Step 4. Developing an action plan for improvement activities

Once improvement activities were identified, an action plan was developed to ensure that improvement activities were carried out. (See the worked example in Table 12.1.)

Priority Improvement Matrix – 10 principles of good practice

Best practice indicator	1	2	3	4	5
1. Planning	✓				
2. Leadership					
3. Equity	✓				
4. Learner		✓	✓		
5. Design					
6. Staff					
7. Technical					
8. Improvement					
9. Administration	✓				
10. Support					

✓ indicates improvement priority

This matrix is included to assist course teams identify and prioritize improvement opportunities. Improvement teams can identify improvement activities by checking each of the four to five indicators in each of the categories.

Improvement Priorities – Business Studies Department
1. Develop a realistic costing of the development costs for the online delivery of Accounting 1.
2. Survey both mainstream and online delivery of Accounting 1 students and compare the extent of student satisfaction with their course.

Figure 12.2   *A worked example of the use of the Improvement Matrix in developing a good practice framework for online delivery*

Below we present the best practice framework for online delivery as adapted in the case study.

Principle 1. Good practice for online delivery involves informed planning and management of resources

Policies and mission statements adopted by online projects must include reference to teaching and learning strategies.

Online delivery ensures that trained people, infrastructure and facilities are available and adequate for each project.

Table 12.1 *Example of a departmental action plan*

Good practice indicator The objective	Strategy/activity How?	Target/indicator How will we know when we have achieved the objective?	Due date When?	Accountability Who?
A realistic costing of all aspects of online delivery has been made including the efficient and equitable allocation of all departmental resources	1. All costs are identified and allocated to an online account 2. Costs are analysed and efficiency measures implemented 3. Partnership activities explored	The department can establish the exact cost of delivering an online programme to 200 students	Oct	Head of Department
Qualitative and quantitative performance indicators have been identified	Client satisfaction surveys developed and implemented for both online and mainstream courses	Client satisfaction surveys indicate positive trend to satisfaction with online courses	June–Oct	Course Team

Indicators of good practice

1. Planning for online delivery is integrated with all planning activities within the faculty/department, including financial, human resource and support service planning.
2. An improvement plan identifying responsibilities, performance indicators and critical processes has been developed and is monitored to evaluate online programmes.
3. A realistic costing of all aspects of online delivery has been made including the efficient and equitable allocation of all departmental resources.
4. Online policies and processes have been incorporated into the organization's quality system.
5. Projects are regularly reviewed and opportunities identified are acted upon.

Principle 2. Good practice for online delivery involves sustained, committed leadership

Leadership style and behaviour are critical in ensuring that the organization's goals for online delivery are achieved.

Institutional support for the development and use of online activities is a critical prerequisite for their widespread adoption and integration into mainstream programmes.

Indicators of good practice

1. Staff in leadership roles demonstrate commitment to the provision and maintenance of online activities and ongoing improvement processes.
2. Strategies have been implemented to provide a level of complex technical and online support required to run efficient, reliable and 'user friendly' systems.
3. Collaborative arrangements with other faculties and departments and/or with other educational institutions and/or with industry have been explored to ensure effective access to and use of resources.
4. The impact of online projects and their outcomes on existing managerial, administrative and physical facilities have been assessed.

Principle 3. Good practice for online delivery involves improving access for all clients, incorporates equity and promotes cultural diversity

The provision of online projects improves the access, participation and success rates of under-represented groups.

Learning opportunities ensure that learners are not limited in their engagement due to physical location, disability, race, ethnicity, level of technological skills or level of access to physical resources and that their level of language and literacy skills is taken into account. Appropriate access to the outcomes of online delivery is available to all students irrespective of income and location. Online delivery actively encourages the diversity of student groups.

Indicators of good practice

1. Barriers that prevent current and potential students accessing online delivery products and services are identified and strategies to improve access and participation are implemented.
2. Existing data from the Pro-Vice-Chancellor Academic Services and Equity's office is used to identify and develop specific strategies for targeted equity groups.
3. Courseware development for online delivery accommodates the background, skills and interests of equity groups.
4. Delivery media are selected on the basis of 'best fit' between learner effectiveness, accessibility and cost.
5. Programmes avoid prohibitive attendance requirements, unnecessary control of the pace of learning, or restrictions on entry and exit options.

Principle 4. Good practice for online delivery involves understanding the requirements of the learner and reflects stakeholder requirements

The main focus of online developments is the needs of learners, clients and stakeholders. Online delivery has a student-centred approach that is soundly based in an understanding of learners' characteristics and needs. Stakeholder requirements are reflected in the provision of online projects.

Indicators of good practice

1. External and internal clients and stakeholders have been identified (eg, government agencies, community groups) and their needs and expectations are reflected in online delivery processes.
2. Online delivery policies and practices make clear the organization's obligations to its learners and the learners' obligations to the institution.
3. An appropriate range of resources is available to accommodate student learning.
4. A process for assessing customer requirements and satisfaction is developed and implemented.

Principle 5. Good practice in online delivery involves the design, development and implementation of programmes for effective and active learning

Course design, development and implementation processes are sufficiently rigorous to ensure that courses meet the requirements of learners, industry and the professions and are effective in achieving learning outcomes.

Indicators of good practice

Course design, development and assessment

1. Course design incorporates interactive instruction techniques mediated by human intervention and a supportive learning environment.
2. Programme and course objectives clearly specify the subject matter to be covered, the intellectual skills to be acquired and the learning methods used.
3. Course design processes reflect desired graduate attributes, promote active learning and recognize varied starting points in levels of confidence, learning styles and motivation.
4. Criteria for evaluating student performance are clearly established, stated in course guidelines and are generally understood by students and staff.
5. Online project outcomes are regularly benchmarked against learning outcomes in mainstream courses to ensure consistency.

Principle 6. Good practice in online delivery involves creating confident and committed staff with new competencies

Recruitment and management processes provide development opportunities for all staff to ensure that they have the skills to meet client-focused and equitable outcomes.

Indicators of good practice

1. Formal or informal professional development for online delivery activities (including subject, technical and instructional design expertise) are identified and systematically implemented.
2. Changes to staff roles and work practices as a result of changes to teaching and learning are recognized, processes are in place to inform the human resources department and to address potential industrial relations issues.
3. Good practice of online delivery is both rewarded and effectively disseminated to all staff across the organization.

4. Procedures and incentives are in place to encourage staff to make appropriate and innovative use of electronic information resources to improve the academic programme, publish scholarly information, and to encourage equitable student use.
5. Where relevant, staff work plans incorporate the staff's professional development needs for the development, delivery and support of online courses.

Principle 7. Good practice in online delivery involves managing and maintaining the technical infrastructure

Decisions about the choice of technology are driven by consideration of learners' needs, the ability of teachers and other staff to provide support for learners, and the curriculum content of the programme. Resource materials are of sound quality, suitable for the purpose, and well matched with technologies and with staffing requirements.

Indicators of good practice

1. The choice of technology, including the delivery method, reflects learners needs, the curriculum content of the programme and human resource availability.
2. The technology is supported by a faculty technology plan that includes:
   - how the technology is to be used for learning;
   - how people are to be trained to use the technology;
   - how the technology is to be managed and maintained.
3. Information technology standards are in place and members of online projects are aware of these so that they can make an informed choice when purchasing technology.
4. Decisions have been made on whether any technology is required for the programme, and the preferred technology or mix of technologies to satisfy requirements has been identified and prioritized.
5. Decisions have been made on whether to buy-in or adapt existing learning materials or to develop new materials.

Principle 8. Good practice for online delivery involves evaluating for continuous improvement

Online delivery evaluates and continuously improves its provision of flexible delivery. Online initiatives are continuously informed by the evaluation of learning outcomes, equity considerations, cost-effectiveness and stakeholder satisfaction.

Indicators of good practice

1. Qualitative and quantitative performance indicators have been identified for workers and disadvantaged groups.
2. Online delivery processes and outcomes are regularly benchmarked against other departments or institutions.
3. Online delivery provides for formal investigations and specific action to deal with student complaints (see student complaint policy).

Principle 9. Good practice for online delivery involves the provision of effective and efficient administrative systems and services

The institution provides administrative systems and services that support and complement the provision of online delivery.

Indicators of good practice

1. Management information systems are flexible and take into account all aspects of online delivery including student enrolment, production scheduling, delivery processes, planning and costing mechanisms and meet the demands of online delivery in terms of time frames, reliability and accessibility.
2. Administrative processes facilitate learner progress while allowing maximum flexibility in programme choice.
3. There is ready electronic access to information resources such as bulletin boards, with sufficient capacity to supply high-volume data where appropriate.
4. The copyright and intellectual property implications of buying, licensing or developing materials have been explored and processes are in place conforming with organization policy.

Principle 10. Good practice in online delivery involves supporting the needs of learners

The needs for student learning, technical and personal support for online delivery are identified, provided for and regularly reviewed. Decisions on the comprehensiveness of services depend on the purposes of online delivery and the diversity of its student body.

Indicators of good practice

1. Online delivery systematically studies the characteristics of its student cohort and identifies the support needs of the student population.

2. Online delivery has an organized system for admission, assessment, orientation, support and student follow-up compatible with the circumstances of students.

3. Support services are provided to enable all students to participate effectively and to enhance their success in achieving their educational outcomes.

4. Educational programmes address the differing skill levels of users, and strategies are implemented to provide online help and support.

5. A decision has been made about the extent to which equipment will be provided to learners (eg, on loan, or by access in a library) and the extent to which equipment must be provided for staff use.

6. Precise, accurate and current information is readily available and well publicized to students concerning:
   (a) educational outcomes;
   (b) degrees, curricular offerings;
   (c) the total costs of online delivery modules;
   (d) other financial obligations, student financial aid and fee refund policies;
   (e) requirements for admission;
   (f) requirements for achievement of degrees;
   (g) assessment processes;
   (h) rules defining inappropriate student conduct and the redress of grievances.

Section IV: THE FUTURE

Chapter 13

Anticipating tomorrow's innovations

In this concluding chapter we shift our attention from the present to the future. We try to anticipate the directions of change. We consider, first, the changes that we are likely to see in the field of education and training. We then consider the likely developments in the area of technology. We conclude by underscoring the importance of maintaining a focus on learning and all that that implies.

What are the forces driving change?

Trends in education and training

The picture often painted is that developments in computer and communications technology are about to transform completely the way in which education and training are delivered.

There can be no doubt that the shift to digitally delivered resource-based learning represents one of the most radical changes we have seen in post-secondary education. It is also quite apparent that there is widespread interest among teachers and trainers in the possibilities that are offered by interactive multimedia and online delivery. It is also true that the more sophisticated and simple-to-use digital technologies become, the more that teachers will be attracted to taking advantage of the potential that these technologies offer for distance education delivery. However, it is an enormous leap in logic to move from saying that digital delivery is being taken up apace to saying that the electronic delivery of courses will make more traditional modes of delivery obsolete. Education and training have been surprisingly resistant to wholesale change in the past. How realistic therefore is the picture of change that is being painted?

How do experts see delivery modes changing?

In a modified Delphi study involving a group of 198 Australian university staff with interest and expertise in information technology, Hesketh *et al.* (1996) asked respondents to identify forces for change in the next five years. In order of their perceived importance, the factors identified were:

- student need for flexible delivery to fit in with lifestyles;
- competition among universities in attracting undergraduate, postgraduate and continuing professional development students;
- a perception that other competing universities have a technological edge;
- opportunities to export education more readily to overseas countries;
- expectations from the business sector and professional bodies that students will be literate in the use of technology;
- the possibility that the federal government will provide incentives for computer-mediated communication in teaching;
- students' level of expectation that computer-mediated communication will be used in teaching;
- the threat to Australian universities from marketing in Australia by overseas universities;
- the potential for computer-mediated communication to provide more equitable access to education for some disadvantaged groups;
- the possibility that industry and professional bodies will provide accredited degrees if universities do not meet their needs.

In the same study the investigators asked which technologies were most likely to be adopted within the next five years. Respondents replied:

- students will have the facility to log on remotely and conduct online searches of libraries and other research databases;
- e-mail will serve as a communication medium between staff and students;
- courses will be delivered using traditional methods;
- students will have online access to course materials – lecture notes, overheads, computer-based learning materials;
- traditional lectures will incorporate widespread use of computer-mediated presentation techniques;
- electronic communication will be used to facilitate collaborative group work.

The striking feature of this list is that the predictions it offers seem so plausible. In a field that is noted for hyperbole, it is to say the least surprising to find that the champions of the digital delivery media see a future that is not greatly different from what we all expect anyway. This is in spite of the fact that the respondents were in many cases in the vanguard of those championing change.

If we want to understand the reasons the winds of change are blowing in this direction, then we need to focus on the forces driving change rather than its chaotic nature.

As the country that is still responsible for most of the advances in digital technology, the United States is also the country that sees the greatest potential in the development of information technology for education. However, most of this increase is expected to be accounted for by the growth in demand for lifelong learning. Most will be tied to workplace requirements. The learners who are expected to be the main beneficiaries of the shift to digital delivery are therefore people who are working; they will be mature learners. They will be learners who are studying part-time and who are non-residential. These students already make up the majority of the post-secondary education student body.

We need to be particularly cautious in predicting the impact that the shift to digital delivery will have at the technical and vocational level. The greatest threat to government-funded institutions is in the fields of workplace training and continuing professional development. Around the world, the vocational education and training sector has been moving towards a competency-based model. Initially, attention was focused on the specification of required competencies. However, more recently attention has shifted towards the methods used to assess the acquisition of competencies. This shift in attention has in turn resulted in a shift in focus from teaching to assessment.

Concurrent with the introduction of competency-based training, governments have opened up the training market to private providers. The effect of this could be to strip the courseware development out of the institutional providers and to focus effort on assessment. This overlooks a factor that is not so often taken into account by educational innovators but which is well understood by educational policy makers. This is that the programmes in the vocational education and training sector frequently substitute for unemployment. By convincing or obliging those who are unemployed to take up training, governments can artificially lower the unemployment statistics, bolstering their reputation for economic management. For people who undertake training as an alternative to unemployment, the social interaction that is possible on-campus is likely to make this a more attractive option than studying in isolation. Distance education is favoured more by people who are already employed and who need a mode of study that fits in with their family commitments.

The largest distance education providers have refined their production processes to the point that they achieve maximum efficiency for the media. They are able to do that by relying on teaching strategies that are appropriate for the market size. As we have pointed out, the shift to interactive multimedia and online delivery is not likely to make providers much more efficient. The most feasible way in which institutions can exploit the potential of multimedia in the changing market place is not in the creation of whole programmes but in the development of small segments of programmes. In tackling the task they need to put greater effort into the design and development of materials and into understanding the teaching–learning processes that are involved in online delivery.

It would not be reasonable to expect that the principles that apply to print-based distance education and to face-to-face teaching will all be equally applicable to the knowledge media. Tapping the full potential of these media is likely to involve the application of principles of which we are not yet aware. If a full understanding of the potential of these media can only be gained through research and the process of trial and error, then we should not expect that this understanding will be arrived at overnight.

The advance of digital technology

It is a rash person indeed who is prepared to forecast more than three years ahead what is going to happen in the field of information technology. Nevertheless, if you are about to embark on re-equipping your organization as part of the first stage of making the transition to the knowledge media, then it would be comforting to have some foreknowledge of the areas where the most far-reaching changes are likely to occur. While we may not be able to anticipate individual developments, we can, with a considerable degree of confidence, anticipate a number of general trends. To do this we need to understand the main factors responsible for change. These are the factors that are contributing to the increase in the basic capabilities of microcomputers:

- the falling cost and increasing capacity of computer memory;
- the falling cost and increasing capacity of disk storage media;
- the increasing speed of microprocessors;
- the trend towards digitizing all forms of information;
- developments in compression technology.

Let us first examine how each of these factors has contributed to the way digital technology has been advancing.

Increasing memory capacity

There is a rough rule of thumb that is recognized in the computer industry that says that computer memory halves in price and doubles in capacity every 18 months. This is known as Moore's Law. While the downward trend in the cost of memory may not have tracked a straight-line path, over time the relationship has held. We can confirm this by comparing the present cost of memory with the cost some years ago.

The cost of computer memory and disk storage has been steadily falling ever since computers were first invented. RAM chips cost approximately $1 per byte in 1975. By 2000 they will be less than $1 per megabyte. However, the fact that memory has become more affordable does not in itself account for the rapid development in the capability of computers. Rather it has been the fact that the increase in memory capacity at falling cost has allowed more functions to be shifted onto computers, and because the way in which functions are performed has become increasingly sophisticated.

Increasing disk storage capacity

The cost of disk storage is about one-hundredth the cost of memory storage. However, the cost of disk storage has been falling at approximately the same rate as the cost of memory storage. In 1985 a hard drive capacity cost approximately $500 per megabyte. By 2000, one megabyte of hard drive capacity will cost less than a cent.

The arrival of the CD ROM was the development that was foreshadowed as opening the door to the world of multimedia. It certainly achieved this. Yet no sooner have CD ROM drives become standard in desktop computers than the capacity limitations of this medium have been reached. When the CD ROM drive first appeared, most desktop computers were sold with drives of 100 Mb capacity – one-sixth of the capacity of a CD ROM. Now the standard drive is 4 or 6 Gb – up to ten times the capacity of a CD ROM.

The limits of hard drive and memory capacity are set by manufacturing methods. That is why manufacturers have been able to increase the capacity of hard drives and memory so rapidly. However, replacement of the CD ROM requires the establishment of a new set of standards and achieving agreement on standards takes much longer than reducing the manufacturing tolerances on a production line.

Developments have also taken place at regular intervals in the technologies of removable storage media. The original eight-inch floppy diskettes gave way to five-and-a-half-inch floppy diskettes which in turn gave way to three-and-a-quarter inch micro diskettes. Now the ZIP disk and the super disk vie with each other as the next standard, with yet another contender waiting in the wings. Here again, the need for establishment of standards has been the factor that has most governed the pace of change.

Increasing processor speed

Even with increased memory and storage capacity the capabilities of computers is being stretched, resulting in demands for increasing processor speed. Digital video for example needs to be compressed to fit onto available storage media. Replaying digital video normally involves concurrent decompression of the video files which requires high processing speed to produce the desired result.

The amount of processing involved in decompression depends on the size of the image and the frame rate. Replaying full-screen full-motion video requires considerable digital processing power. The improvement in processor speed has led to a rapid and very obvious improvement in the quality of video reproduction.

However, this improvement in video reproduction is largely limited to the replay of video from local disks. The communication speed possible over remote access connections is already the major rate-limiting factor in real-time delivery over the Internet. While compression technology has allowed the development of real-time streaming video, the limited capacity of the public networks puts an upper limit on the amount of data that can be moved from place to place in a given time. This restriction is unlikely to be eased in the near future.

Local delivery of video is not constrained in the way that Internet distribution is because within organizations re-cabling and re-equipping is a feasible option.

Digitization of information

The invention of the laser printer enabled type to be digitized and led to the creation of desktop publishing. The development of the CD heralded the transition to digitization of audio recording. The last remaining hurdle to be overcome has been the digitization of video – and that is now happening.

The factor that held back the introduction of digital video was the capacity restriction of available storage media. Increases in media capacity have relieved this restriction to some extent. However, the amount of storage capacity required to hold full-length feature productions was much greater than can be provided in the short term by improvements in media capacity. What has enabled the breakthrough has been the development of compression technology.

Advances in compression technology

The single function that defines the field of interactive multimedia is the ability that computers now have to replay digital video. All of the other functions that go to make up interactive multimedia have been possible for many years – graphics, animation, sound and branching presentation. However, it is only as a result of the recent developments in technology that computers have acquired the ability to handle video.

Video compression technology was originally developed to enable video conferences to be conducted over narrow bandwidth communication links. (When we speak of 'narrow' in this context, the term is being used relatively. Narrow bandwidth is comparative. Broadcast video requires 30 megabits per second. Compressed video conferencing required 56 Kilobits per second (Kbps). A data rate of 56 Kbps has only recently been achievable via modem.) Once video compression became available it was recognized that this technology offered a solution to the problem of storing digitized video as well.

Video compression enabled the size of a video clip to be reduced down to as little as a tenth of its original size. However, this was still very large. Other techniques were therefore used to further reduce the amount of data in video files, including reducing the size of the image, the frame rate and the number of colours.

In recent years video compression has found much wider use in the production of CD ROMs. The same type of technology is now being used to send and receive audio transmissions over the Internet.

The introduction of video compression technology greatly reduced the amount of disk storage capacity needed to hold a given amount of compressed video. However, decompressing the compressed video involved a prodigious amount of computation. Initially, microprocessors in desktop computers did not have the power to decompress video. This problem was originally solved by equipping computers with a plug-in video card which had its own digital signal processors for compressing and decompressing digitized video. As the speed of micro-processors increased, it became more practicable for the main processor to take over the role of the video processor and for decompression to be done in software.

The net effect

What has been the combined effect of these five key factors?

The most important effect has been to increase enormously the amount of information that can be stored and processed and to allow the size, and therefore the sophistication, of pieces of software to be greatly increased.

The second major effect has been to enable computers to acquire the ability to process an increasing variety of information.

There is every reason to believe that these trends will continue. Future advances in information technology will be driven by the removal of restrictions on storage and the speeding up of even quite complex processing tasks. The area where changes will be occurring most rapidly in the immediate future will be in digital video recording. As the restrictions on processing and storage are removed, the ability of computers will quickly eclipse the capabilities of analogue technology. The most important development on the immediate horizon is the arrival of a new storage medium.

What's on the horizon?

DVD *optical disk technology*

It is only in the last couple of years that CD ROM drives have become more or less standard in desktop computers. Yet already a new storage system has appeared on the market which will soon begin to make CD ROM obsolete.

Over the past year, a new type of home entertainment unit has appeared in the consumer electronics market: the digital video disc (DVD) player. These players look very like CD players but they replay video rather than audio. (They can replay audio CDs as well.)

DVD video players use the same type of laser technology as found in CD players but take a new type of optical disc. This disc differs from CDs in three respects:

- It is 'read' with a higher frequency laser which enables data to be stored much more densely than on a conventional CD.
- It can store data on both sides.

- Each side of the disc can have two recording layers. (This is achieved by using a semi-transparent upper layer.)

These three differences together give DVD video discs a maximum capacity of 17 gigabytes (Gb) compared with 0.6 Gb for a CD; that is, seven times the capacity of a CD. DVD video players also include MPEG video compression. This allows the available storage capacity to be used much more efficiently.

The combined effect of the increase in actual storage capacity and the improvement in the efficiency with which the capacity is used allows full-length, full-screen, full-motion video recordings to be fitted onto a single DVD video disc. DVD video discs represent one of three new optical disc recording standards based on DVD technology. The other two standards are: DVD ROM – for computer data, and DVD audio – for high-quality audio recording. The standard for DVD audio has yet to be finalized. DVD optical disks will be available in single-layer single-sided, single-layer double-sided, and double-layer double-sided formats, giving a range of storage capacities from 4.38 Gb.

DVD video is specifically targeted at the home entertainment market. DVD players are expected eventually to replace video disc players and will also partly replace VHS recorders. However, because DVD players will be unable to record video, a significant market for VHS recorders will still remain.

DVD video players offer a large range of features not offered by either video discs or VHS cassettes:

- up to nine different viewpoints (camera angles) can be selected during playback;
- 'seamless' branching;
- up to eight tracks of digital audio.

Because DVD discs are mechanically more robust than video cassettes and are not affected by magnetic fields, they will be a more suitable medium than video cassettes for commercially published educational video titles. However, DVD video is unlikely to be used by educational institutions for in-house production for the foreseeable future.

The production of DVD video involves quite sophisticated editing and compression in order to meet appropriate production standards. The high cost of mastering will make it uneconomic to produce DVD video products for runs of less than several thousand copies. Because of the much greater capacity of DVDs and the added complexity of the mastering processes, the cost of mastering of DVDs is several orders of magnitude higher than the mastering of CDs. This puts this medium out of the range of most educational and training providers. However, DVD will certainly become the standard for commercial publishers and therefore what we are likely to see is educational providers teaming up with commercial publishers for the production of titles for the world market.

Unlike DVD video, DVD ROM technology is certain to play a central role in the in-house development and distribution of courseware. DVD ROM drives are capable of accessing CD ROMs. For a computer manufacturer, swapping from CD ROM drives to DVD ROM drives carries no penalty other than cost. It is cost that is presently delaying the swap-over. Until the amount of software has grown to a level where there is a strong demand for DVD ROM drives there is no reason for manufacturers to reduce their competitiveness by paying the premium for installing DVD. DVD ROM drives have already appeared on the market. The first computers to offer a DVD ROM as standard should soon be emerging.

DVD ROM drives will become available in models offering data recording capability, just as recordable CD ROMs are available today. This is possible because the recording of data is not as technically demanding as recording of high quality video. Recordable DVD ROMs, while still offering the capacity of DVD video, will not involve the same high costs of production. While DVD ROMs cannot be used for recording of high quality video, they may be used for storing multimedia productions.

Most computers equipped with DVD ROM drives are expected to be able to replay DVD video as well as DVD audio, just as computers equipped with CD ROM drives are also able to replay CDs. In looking ahead to the introduction of DVDs, it makes sense for education and training providers to think in terms of using computers equipped with a DVD ROM drive as the standard replay unit for digitally delivered courseware. The integration and standardization of media and replay technology will make it relatively simple to present learners with a standard interface for controlling all media.

Clearing the communications log-jam

Developments in computer technology have been proceeding rapidly. However, developments in communications technology are somewhat slower. The reason for this is not that less investment has been made in telecommunications research but that the field of telecommunications faces certain limits which do not apply in the case of developments in computing.

The first point to realize is that the speed at which public telecommunications networks can be updated is extraordinarily slow. The most important change we have seen in recent years has been the installation of fibre optic cabling throughout major cities. In Australia, the installation of fibre optic cabling began more than a decade ago. Yet the cabling of Australia's cities is still not complete and it will be decades before fibre cabling reaches rural areas. Furthermore, the way in which fibre has been rolled out has been to lay it to the end of streets; the cable that runs down the street is still copper. Australia has one of the most advanced telecommunications networks in the world. It was the first country to begin implementing ISDN and is the country where fast packet switching was invented – yet progress is still slow. In many developing countries, even telephone services are not available to everyone.

The second point to note is that conventional modems have now reached their theoretical speed limit. While we are now starting to see modem manufacturers employing clever tricks such as combining three modems in one to allow an effective functional increase in communication speed, we cannot expect to see the speed of modems increase above 56 Kbps. This means that the only way to obtain an increase in data rate will be to move from dial-up connections to cable.

Software developers are looking at ways of reducing the amount of data that has to be moved around. Compression, already used for video and audio, offers one way of achieving this. However, the increase in traffic on the Internet is principally due to the extensive use of graphics. Another way to alleviate the pressure is to alter the way in which graphics are encoded and stored. It is evident that software developers have begun to recognize the importance of this problem and are taking steps to alleviate it. They are redesigning their graphics packages to use more economical methods of reproduction. Users can also help themselves in this regard. By using graphics judiciously and taking care with the design of their Web sites they can reduce the amount of data that needs to be downloaded and consequently the time spent in waiting for pages to download.

The limitations that apply to the public networks do not apply to local area networks. Recently we have seen a move from 10 Mbps to 100 Mbps ethernet and the replacement of central backbones with faster ATM links. The result is that the quality of on-campus communications can be expected to improve at a faster rate than the quality of communication over the public switched network.

Overcoming the inherent limitations of the Web

When Tim Berners-Lee implemented the Web version of hypertext he left out a number of the features that Ted Nelson had considered essential to effective implementation of the concept. These omissions are now apparent.

Pam (1995) has examined the differences between Xanadu and the Web. He identifies the following as the most crucial:

- Each document is served from a single location with the result that the reliability of the Web is degraded.
- Documents are identified by location (URL) rather than by a unique identifier so that there is no assurance that a document will be available at the location to which a hyperlink is pointing.
- Hyperlinks are embedded within documents rather than within the metadata of the document so that it is only feasible for hyperlinks to point one way.
- Support is not provided for multiple versions of the same document to be publishable as such.
- Support for transclusion (the inclusion of another document by reference to it rather than by copying it) is only provided for images.

Pam considers solutions to these problems are likely to be provided by the development of more advanced Web servers which provide additional features. One such server is Hyperwave, the commercial implementation of the Hyper-G that was originally developed at the University of Graz. Hyperwave is probably the Web server that currently offers the most faithful implementation of Nelson's concept of hypertext. It is able to run on machines using the Microsoft NT or Unix operating systems.

XML

XML stands for 'Extensible Mark-up Language'. It is a new mark-up language that has been developed by the World Wide Web Consortium. It is a greatly simplified dialect of SGML or in other words comprises a subset of SGML commands. It is intended to make SGML usable for distribution of materials on the Web.

As was explained in Chapter 1, HTML is an instance of SGML. It uses a fixed set of commands to format Web pages. While successive versions of HTML have increased the number of commands available, the command set has nevertheless remained fully defined.

XML differs from HTML in that with it you can create your own set of commands or even use data-types that have been created by other users. Already, versions of XML have been created for formatting mathematical text documents showing chemical reactions. It also allows items of information to be given tags that describe their type rather than the format in which the documents should be displayed.

The success of XML depends on the availability of browsers that will understand how to display documents marked up in it. Both Netscape and Microsoft have indicated that they will be supporting the new mark-up language. XML is unlikely to replace HTML for many years because of the large number of documents that are already formatted using this standard. However, the use of HMTL and XML is likely to become somewhat differentiated, with HTML being used more for machine-generated documents and XML for authored documents.

Authoring systems

Authoring systems provide the keys that unlock the power of computers for use in interactive multimedia in education and training.

The major developments being seen in the area of course authoring software are related to ease of use and the migration of interactive multimedia to the Web. All suppliers of authoring systems are moving quickly to enable their products to distribute courseware over the Web and many new developers are appearing with Web authoring products.

Suppliers of authoring systems are trying to streamline, simplify and speed up the process of courseware authoring. This reduces the cost of authoring and attracts more users into the market. It can be expected that this process will continue with increasing efforts.

Most authoring software still places greater importance on presentation and ease of use than on pedagogical features. For the education and training providers to realize the savings for which they are hoping, online delivery systems will need to address the issue of electronic feedback and assessment.

Development of standards for interactive multimedia delivery

One of the most enticing prospects that recent advances in interactive multimedia hold out to us is that of being able to customize the delivery of education and training to the needs of the learner. The possibility exists of providing learners with learning opportunities that take into account their learning styles and which are matched to their rate of learning. Yet the attainment of this ideal is being thwarted by the proliferation of incompatible learning systems and materials that can only be used in specific environments.

How does one ensure that courseware developed for one platform and one authoring package can be supported by an interactive learning environment provided by a different supplier and running on a different platform? Should the choice of learning management system limit the range of courseware upon which one can draw? Clearly this is not desirable. What are needed if this situation is to be avoided are sets of standards that guarantee the inter-operability of systems that adhere to the standards.

Such standards are presently being developed by the consortium of education institutions called EDUCAUSE, formed by the merger of CAUSE and EDUCOM under the National Learning Infrastructure Initiative (Twigg, 1994). They are defined in the Instructional Management Systems (IMS) Project. The goal of the project is to enable an open learning architecture for learning with digital media. The way the project has set out to achieve this goal is through the promulgation of a technical specification for learning materials and systems and the implementation of a proof of concept (EDUCOM, 1998).

The IMS specification has been preceded by the development of a set of core assumptions and requirements related to online learning systems and online courseware. The assumptions have been refined through focus groups, conferences and other interactions with prospective end-users as well as through discussions with the technical developer community.

The IMS project is focused on providing a standard way of delivering and managing information common in learning interchanges. The vision of those responsible for guiding the project is to create a standard for developers of high-quality materials for an interactive learning environment. Learning materials that are easy to use, inter-operable and capable of customization to an individual learner's needs will be able to be developed. A learner will be able to track a personalized pathway through a learning programme.

EDUCAUSE argues that the IMS standard will advance the field of educational multimedia development by bringing about:

- lower cost development and deployment of learning materials;
- improved quality of online learning materials and environments;
- greater access to learning opportunities;
- more customized learning experiences.

The promulgation of the IMS specification is not intended to stifle innovation in the development of interactive multimedia systems. It is not expected to lead to a situation in which all multimedia systems offer the same set of features.

While the IMS project is specifically addressing the needs of the education and training community in the United States, the influence of the specification is likely to extend worldwide.

The impact of educational and technical change

It is a cliché that we live in an age of rapid change. Nevertheless, both the environment of education and the means of educating are changing rapidly and significantly. Rapid change generates an ongoing need for retraining and lifelong learning. This in turn leads to a changing clientele for post-compulsory education – a clientele who demand flexible forms of delivery responsive to their economic and social circumstances. It leads to demands for a 'just-in-time' approach to educational delivery: the delivery of small segments of learning when and where the need arises. In the case of higher education for full-time students, changes to educational delivery may continue to be at the margins. The use of instructional technology will continue to be complementary and supplementary to traditional forms of delivery. However, the new clientele will demand a flexibility in delivery for which the knowledge media has the potential to provide better solutions.

The options available to education and training providers will depend upon the nature of technological developments. The immediate developments in technology will be centred on the convergence of computer and communications technologies. Advances will be most evident and most rapid in the area of integration of video into the environment of multimedia. The adoption of DVD, improvements in compression technologies and increases in processor speed will all make a contribution here. While advances can also be expected in the area of data communications, the pace of development there will be slower because of the delay represented by the time taken to put in place new communications infrastructure. Developments in software will greatly increase the ease with which the capabilities of digital technology can be exploited. Together, these technological developments will offer greatly increased flexibility in meeting the educational and training demands of tomorrow's world.

In the end, the purpose of the delivery enterprise is supporting learning

Fifty years ago, distance education (or 'correspondence education' as it was then known) was regarded as very much a second-best mode of delivery: failure rates were high; non-completion rates were even higher; and the reputation of this mode of delivery was poor.

The success of the UK Open University altered educators' perceptions of what was possible in distance education. Attention paid to the needs of learners led to pass rates increasing. The reputation of distance education rose to the point where, if it was not always seen as the equal of face-to-face teaching, it was certainly considered a respectable mode of delivery.

Fifteen years ago, distance education providers began exploring the potential of technology to support the delivery of programmes. They started simply with e-mail; moved on to computer-managed learning; and recently began entering the field of online delivery. Today, distance education, far from being regarded as a second-best mode of delivery, is held up as the way of the future.

Nevertheless, there is a risk that in rushing to embrace the benefits that digital technologies offer, we can lose sight of the primary goal — improving student learning. The message we have tried to convey throughout this book is that the true potential of the knowledge media lies not so much in lowering the costs of educational delivery but in enhancing the quality of the student's learning experience.

Taking advantage of economies of scale to increase the rate of recovery of the investment in courseware development, forming consortia of providers to lower the costs of development and make electronic delivery more affordable, are worthwhile undertakings. However, the primary reason for choosing to use technology in the first place ought to be to facilitate learning more effectively.

Communications technology offers the potential to deliver programmes more economically, to deliver them to a wider market, to increase interaction, to increase the range of ways in which we teach, and even to make learning more fun. The convergence of technology offers the possibility of achieving advances that go beyond the wildest dreams of those who first conceived of the concepts of hypertext, annotation systems, computer-assisted instruction and computer-managed learning. However, technology is seductive. Without realizing it we can allow the application of technology to become the end rather than the means of delivering digitally.

In considering what current advances in delivery technology have to offer distance education, we need to keep at the forefront of our considerations the recognition that at the core of the educational experience there are teachers and there are learners. Without the committed participation of these parties in the education and training contexts, whatever contribution technology may have to make will count for nothing. The value of the advances we are seeing in digital technology lies in the extent to which they enable teachers to do more effectively and efficiently those things that will enable students to learn.

Glossary

In this glossary, *italics* are used for terms that have their own entry.

Anonymous FTP   A form of FTP service that allows users to log on to a file server without providing a password to gain access. It is used to make collections of files such as collections of shareware software generally available to Internet users.

Applet   Literally 'little applications'; small programs written in Java programming language that are downloaded from a *Web server* and run inside a *Web browser*. Applets are generally written to provide functions that cannot readily be provided using *HTML*.

Asynchronous   Occurring at different times; in relation to communication, interaction in which the parties each participate at different times.

Asynchronous conferencing   A form of computer conferencing in which participants do not interact at the same time. Contributions to the conference are generally posted to a conferencing system which arranges the contributions by topic or by time of receipt and makes them available to other participants.

Asynchronous Transfer Mode (ATM)   A communication standard for broadband–ISDN transmission capable of supporting data rates of up to 600 Mbits/s.

Australian Quality Awards   A programme designed to support business excellence in Australian organizations to increase international competitiveness using self-assessment as a tool. Many countries around the world have similar programmes, eg the Baldrige Award in the United States.

Bandwidth   The transmission capacity of a telecommunications link. In the case of digital communications, bandwidth is measured in terms of bits per second. The greater the bandwidth the greater the volume of information that can be transmitted over the link in a given period of time.

Benchmarking   The concept of benchmarking that has been adopted in this book is: the on–going systematic process of measuring and comparing the work processes of one organization with the those of another. The purpose of benchmarking is to provide a point of reference for evaluating the improvement in a process.

Best practice The adoption of work practices which, when effectively linked together, can be expected to lead to sustainable world-class outcomes in quality, customer satisfaction, flexibility, timeliness, innovation and cost-competitiveness.

Browser See *Web client*.

Cable modem A modem which connects to metropolitan cable services. Installing a cable modem may require taking out a subscription to a cable television service. This provides a high speed connection from homes and businesses. However, the cost of installation and use is high and the service is only available in districts that have been cabled for television.

CAL See *computer-assisted learning*.

CERN The European Laboratory for Particle Physics, a collective of high-energy physics researchers. This was where the idea for the World Wide Web was conceived. It was originally developed as a way of transporting research information throughout the organization.

Chat See *synchronous* conferencing.

CML See *computer-managed learning*.

Collaborative tools See *asynchronous* conferencing, *synchronous* conferencing.

Computer-assisted learning (CAL) Learning that is facilitated via computer. In the past this would have been referred to as 'computer-assisted instruction'.

Computer-managed learning (CML) A form of *computer-assisted learning* in which the computer is used to manage the pace and sequence in which a learner proceeds through a course. The concept of CML originated from early attempts at obtaining the benefits of computers without incurring the high costs. CML systems delivered computer-scored tests and directed a student's learning, but the learning materials were delivered via other media, usually print.

Courseware The digital material designed to facilitate learning of behaviours, understanding, attitudes and/or propensities. It usually refers to materials that cover a topic, module or unit.

CQAHE The Committee for Quality Assurance in Higher Education (Australia).

Distance education A mode of study in which students rarely, if ever, participate in face-to-face interaction and both instruction and support are provided via learning packages or synchronous forms of delivery mediated by technology.

DVD ROM Successor to the CD ROM. It uses the same optical technology but can record at a much higher density owing to use of a higher frequency laser and a dual-layer, double-sided platter. Like CD ROMs, DVD ROMs will be available in both read-only and write-once versions.

Economies of scale Economies that arise from increasing the size of an operation; in the case of distance education, economies that arise from increasing the numbers of students entering an institution or entering a subject.

Effectiveness When used in relation to courseware, the term 'effectiveness' refers to the ability to effect changes in the learner's understanding, skills, competencies, attitudes and dispositions.

Efficiency Efficiency relates to the minimization of resource consumption (or possibly the maximization of return on investment). When used in relation to education, the term 'efficiency' implies having the desired effect but it does not imply maximizing effectiveness. Where efficiency is the goal, a balance must be struck between costs and benefits.

Ethernet   A local area network system originally developed at Xerox Palo Alto Research Center and later made a standard. Ethernets operate at 10 Mbps over coaxial cable and link computers and servers in 'daisy-chain' fashion.

Expert system   Computer-based systems in which the knowledge of a field is captured as a knowledge base. An inference engine allows conclusions to be drawn based on a given set of assumptions.

Extensible Mark-up Language (XML)   The adaptation of *SGML* that is expected to replace *HTML* as the mark-up language for authored text on the Web. Unlike *HTML*, it has the capacity to support the definition of new formats and is therefore much more versatile than *HTML*.

Digital delivery   Delivery of courses via the World Wide Web, interactive multimedia, and any other medium in which information is carried in digital form.

File Transfer Protocol   A widely-used protocol for transferring files across networks.

Flexible delivery   The provision of learning experiences in a variety of ways (eg, face-to-face, workplace, print, interactive multimedia) that are responsive to learners' needs.

Flexible learning   The offering of learning experiences using media or combinations of media that provide time, place and pace flexibility for learners.

Formative evaluation   Evaluation which is undertaken for the purpose of monitoring the progress of a project. It may involve either gathering information on components of a project as they are developed or tracking a project through its pilot stage.

FTP   See *File Transfer Protocol*.

HTML   See *Hyper Text Mark-up Language*.

Hyperlink   Connections between hypertext documents.

Hypermedia   Hypertext that includes other media.

Hypertext   Text that, when selected, results in the retrieval of other documents.

HyperText Mark-up Language (HTML)   The formatting language used to create documents for the World Wide Web.

Integrated electronic learning environment   A system that provides a comprehensive range of learning support services such as courseware delivery, e-mail, conferencing, computer-scored testing, and learning management. Examples of commercially-available electronic learning environments include FirstClass, Learning Space, The Learning Manager, TopClass and WebCT.

Integrated Services Digital Network (ISDN)   A high-speed public network that is able to carry voice, data and video. In its basic configuration it offers two transmission speeds: 56 kbps and 1 Mbps. However, two or more 56 Kbps channels can be coupled to provide intermediate speeds.

Internet   A collection of networks and computers that has evolved from a couple of computers 30 years ago into a loosely connected global network comprising thousands of smaller regional networks. It allows users to exchange information in a wide variety of forms.

Intranet   A network internal to an organization.

ISDN   See *Integrated Services Digital Network*.

Knowledge media   A collective term referring to the World Wide Web and interactive multimedia.

Listserv   A program that maintains mailing lists, automatically receiving and sending messages to members of the list. A person who has subscribed to a listserv can mail to the other members of the list by sending an e-mail message to the listserv. A listserv can also place new members on the list and remove members from a list automatically upon request.

MIME   See *Multi-purpose Internet Mail Extensions*.

MOO   See *Multi-user dimension Object-Oriented*.

Mosaic   The first publicly available *Web browser*. Mosaic was commercialized as Netscape Navigator.

Moving Pictures Experts Group (MPEG)   The term generally refers to the standards for digital video and audio compression which this group is responsible for developing and promulgating.

Multi-purpose Internet Mail Extensions   A standard for specifying an action that is to take place when a file that has certain characteristics is transferred.

Multi-user dimension *or* **multi-user dungeon (MUD)**   A type of *networked virtual environment* in which the objects are defined by the developer of the environment.

Multi-user dimension Object-Oriented   A type of *networked virtual environment* that is able to be extended by the user.

MUD   See *multi-user dimension*.

Network   A collection of digital devices such as servers, computers and printers that are connected together for the purpose of allowing people to share, store, retrieve and print information.

Networked Virtual Environment (NVE)   Virtual environments created on the Internet.

Open learning   A mode of entry which permits students irrespective of their previous educational achievements to enrol in programmes which offer a measure of flexibility in relation to the time, place, pace and method of study.

PDF   See *Portable Document Format*.

Performance indicators   Quantitative and qualitative descriptors used for assessing performance, eg, the percentage of students who complete a course, the number of times course inquiries are recorded, or a description of the condition that applies when a particular task is completed.

POP   See *Post Office Protocol*.

Portable Document Format (PDF)   A standard for formatting documents developed by Adobe Corporation. Documents that have been stored in PDF format require Adobe Acrobat Viewer for viewing and printing.

Post Office Protocol (POP)   A protocol used by mail client programs for receiving mail from mail servers.

Quality assurance   The totality of the arrangements by which an organization discharges its responsibility for the quality of the teaching it offers, satisfying itself that the mechanisms for quality control are effective and promote improvement.

Quality improvement All of the actions taken throughout the organization to increase the effectiveness and efficiency of activities and processes in order to provide added benefits to both the organization and its clients.

Scaleable systems Systems that are capable of being greatly expanded to support much larger numbers of users.

Self-assessment An internal review by which an organization assesses its own processes and performance against given criteria such as those described in best-practice documents, for example the Australian Business Excellence Framework.

SGML See *Standard Generalized Mark-up Language.*

Simple Mail Transfer Protocol (SMTP) The protocol used by mail servers to exchange mail with other mail servers and by some client mail software to send mail to a mail server.

Standard Generalized Mark-up Language (SGML) A generic language for formatting documents.

Summative evaluation Evaluation which is undertaken for the purpose of providing information in relation to the success of a project. A summative evaluation may be undertaken in order to satisfy the requirements of a funding authority, or to provide information that may be useful in later projects.

Synchronous Occurring at the same time; in relation to communication, interaction involving participation at the same time.

Synchronous conferencing (chat) A form of computer conferencing in which participants interact at the same time. Contributions to the conference are posted to a conferencing server which re-transmits them to other participants in the conferences. Participants may be located in any part of the world. The most widely used form of chat system is Internet Relay Chat (IRC).

Threaded discussions A method of sequencing the contributions to computer conferences by topic. This permits the contributions on a single topic to be reviewed. The alternative method of sequencing contributions is in order of their receipt.

Uniform Resource Locators (URLs) The method of representing hypertext addresses on the World-Wide Web. A URL comprises an initial part specifying the method of action, a second part specifying the address of the computer on which a document or service is located and perhaps further parts specifying the names of files, the port to connect to or the text to search for in a database.

Usenet A global network of news servers.

Web browser A piece of computer software that enables files stored on *Web servers* to be accessed and displayed.

Web client The piece of software that runs on a user's machine to provide an interface to the World Wide Web. The most widely used Web clients are Netscape Navigator and Microsoft Internet Explorer.

Web page The contents of a single *HTML* file.

Web server The software that delivers *Web pages* (*HTML* files) over the World Wide Web.

Web site A collection of *HTML* files (ie, Web pages) made available from a *Web server*.

Xanadu Project The project initiated by Ted Nelson to create a worldwide *hypertext* system. The Xanadu Project was support by Autodesk Corporation for a period.

XML See *Extensible Mark-up Language*.

References

Argyris, C and Schön, D (1974) *Theory in Practice*, Jossey-Bass, San Francisco

Ashenden, D (1987) Costs and Cost Structure in External Studies: A discussion of issues and possibilities in Australian higher education, EIP, Australian Government Publishing Service, Canberra

Atkinson, R and Castro, A (1991) 'The ADENet Project: Improving computer communications for distance education students', in R Atkinson, C McBeath and D Meacham (eds) Quality in Distance Education: ASPESA Forum 91, Bathurst, NSW: Australian and South Pacific External Studies Association (now Open and Distance Learning Association of Australia)

Australian Vice-Chancellors' Committee (1996) Exploiting Information Technology in Higher Education: An issues paper, AV-CC, Canberra <http://www.avcc.edu.au/avcc/pubs/eithe.htm>

Ausubel, D (1963) *The Psychology of Meaningful Verbal Learning*, Grune and Stratton, New York

Bloniarz, PA and Larsen, KR (1997) A Cost/Performance Model for Assessing WWW Service Investments, Centre for Technology in Government, University at Albany, Albany, New York <http://www.ctg.albany.edu>

Boud, D and Feletti, G (1991) (eds) *The Challenge of Problem Based Learning*, Kogan Page, London

Bush, V (1945) As we may think, *Atlantic Monthly*, **176** (1) <http://www.ps.uni-sb.de/~duchier/pub/vbush/>

Committee for Quality Assurance in Higher (1995) Report on 1994 Quality Review, Vol 1 and 2, Australian Government Publishing Service, Canberra

Department of Industrial Relations and Australian Manufacturing Council (1992) International Best Practice: Report on the overseas study mission, Australian Government Publishing Service, Canberra

Drucker, PF (1993) *Post-capitalist Society*, Butterworth-Heinemann, Oxford.

EDUCOM (1998) EDUCOM/NLII Instructional management systems specification document, Version 0.5 <http://educause.edu/program/nlii/nliihome.html>

Evans, T and Nation, D (1989) Dialogue in practice, research and theory in distance education, *Open Learning*, **4** (2)

Flexner, A (1968) *Universities: American, English, German*, originally published in 1930, reprinted by Polity Press, Cambridge

Garrison, DR (1993) 'A cognitive constructivist view of distance education: An analysis of teaching–learning assumptions', *Distance Education*, **14** (2), 199–211

Garrison, DR (1995) 'Constructivism and the role of self-instructional course materials: A reply', *Distance Education*, **16** (1), 136–40

Giddens, A (1991) *Modernity and Self-identity*, Polity Press, Cambridge

Giddens, A (1996) *In Defence of Sociology*, Polity Press, Cambridge

Hesketh, B, Gosper, M, Andrews, J and Sabaz, M (1996) Computer-Mediated Communication in University Teaching, Department of Employment, Education, and Youth Affairs, Canberra

Higher Education Review (1997) Learning for life: Review of higher education financing and policy - A policy discussion paper [West Committee], Australian Government Publishing Service, Canberra

Hiltz, R (1997) Impacts of college-level courses via asynchronous learning networks: Some preliminary results, *Journal of Asynchronous Learning Networks*, **1** (2) <http://www.aln.org/alnweb/journal/jaln_issue1.htm#turoff>

Jones, BJ, Valdez, G, Nowakowski, J and Rasmussen, C (1994) Designing Learning and Technology for Educational Reform, North Central Regional Educational Laboratory, Oak Brook, IL

Kulik, C-L and Kulik, JA (1986) Effectiveness of computer-based education in colleges, *AEDS Journal*, **19**, 81–108

Kulik, C-L and Kulik, JA (1991) Effectiveness of computer-based instruction: An updated analysis, *Computers and Human Behaviour*, **7**, 75–94

Kulik, C-L, Kulik, JA and Cohen, P (1980) Instructional technology and college teaching, *Teaching of Psychology*, **7**, 199–205

Laurillard, D (1993) *Rethinking University Teaching: A framework for the effective use of educational technology*, Routledge, London

May, M (1998) The implications of the Internet for career counselling and the use of career information, *Australian Journal of Career Development*, **7** (1), 24–9

McGill, I and Beaty, L (1992) *Action Learning: A practitioner's guide*, Kogan Page, London

Mitchell, J and Bluer, R (1996) A Planning Model for Innovation. A report for the office of training and further education on new learning technologies: Case studies, Office of Training and Further Education, Melbourne <http://www.otfe.vic.gov.au/about/model/index.htm>

National Board of Employment, Education and Training (1996) Education and Technology Convergence, Commissioned Report No 43, Australian Government Printing Service, Canberra

National Board of Employment, Education and Training, Higher Education Council (1997) Quality in Resource Based Learning, Australian Government Printing Service, Canberra

National Information Infrastructure Taskforce (1994) What it Takes to Make it Happen <http://www.pub.whitehouse.gov/WH/html/library.html>

Newman, JH (1947) *The Idea of a University*, reprinted by Longmans, New York

OECD (1996) Information Technology and the Future for Post-secondary Education, OECD, Paris

Pam, A (1995) Where the World Wide Web Went Wrong, Proceedings of the Asia-Pacific World Wide Web Conference, Sydney <http://www.xanadu.com.au/xanadu/6w-paper.html>

Patterson, G (1989) The Evolution of the University, Occasional Paper No 2, Department of Management, Massey University

Phillips, M, Scott, P and Fage, J (1998) Towards a strategy for the use of new technology in student guidance and support, *Open Learning*, **13** (2), 52–58

Polanyi, M (1958) *Personal Knowledge: Towards a post-critical philosophy*, Routledge & Kegan Paul, London

Polanyi, M (1967) *The Tacit Dimension*, Routledge & Kegan Paul, London

Rumble, G (1997) *Costs and Economics of Open and Distance Learning*, Kogan Page, London

Schiller, N and Cunningham, NA (1998) Delivering course materials to distance learners over the World Wide Web: Statistical data summary, *Journal of Library Services for Distance Education*, **1** (2) <http://www.westga.edu/library/jlsde/>

Schön D (1983) *The Reflective Practitioner: How professionals think in action*, Basic Books, New York

Seely, J, Brown, A and Duguid, CP (1989) Situated cognition and the culture of learning, *Educational Researcher*, **18** (1), 32–42

Stephens, K, Unwin, L and Bolton, N (1997) The use of libraries by postgraduate distance learning students: a mismatch of expectations, *Open Learning*, **12** (4), 25–33

Turoff, M (1997a) Alternative Futures for Distance Learning: The force and the dark side, UNESCO/Open University International Colloquium <http://eies.njit.edu/~turoff/Papers/darkaln.html>

Turoff, M (1997b) Costs for the development of a virtual university, *Journal of Asynchronous Learning Networks*, **1** (1) <http://www.aln.org/alnweb/journal/jaln_issue1.htm#turoff>

Twigg, CA (1994) The need for a national learning infrastructure, *Educom Review*, **29** (4, 5 and 6)

Wagner, P (1994) *A Sociology of Modernity, Liberty and Discipline*, Routledge, London

Index